New Studies in Practical Philosophy

PRACTICAL INFERENCES

New Studies in Practical Philosophy
General Editor: W. D. Hudson

The point of view of this series is that of contemporary analytical philosophy. Each study will deal with an aspect of moral philosophy. Particular attention will be paid to the logic of moral discourse, and the practical problems of morality. The relationship between morality and other 'universes of discourse', such as art and science, will also be explored.

Published:

R. M. Hare, *Practical Inferences*
R. M. Hare, *Essays on Philosophical Method*

Among the titles in preparation are:
R. M. Hare, *Essays on the Moral Concepts*
R. M. Hare, *Applications of Moral Philosophy*

PRACTICAL INFERENCES

R. M. HARE
*White's Professor of Moral Philosophy
in the University of Oxford*

UNIVERSITY OF CALIFORNIA PRESS
Berkeley and Los Angeles   1972

UNIVERSITY OF CALIFORNIA PRESS

Berkeley and Los Angeles, California

ISBN: 0-520-02179-7

Library of Congress Catalog Card Number: 70-182287

© R. M. Hare 1971 except where stated

All rights reserved. No part of this publication
may be reproduced or transmitted, in any form
or by any means, without permission.

Contents

	Editor's Foreword	vi
	Preface	vii
	Acknowledgements	viii
1	Imperative Sentences (1949)	1
	Appendix: Extract from 'Practical Reason'	22
2	Some Alleged Differences between Imperatives and Indicatives (1967)	25
3	Wanting: Some Pitfalls (1968)	44
4	Practical Inferences (1969)	59
5	Meaning and Speech Acts (1970)	74
	Appendix: Reply to Mr G. J. Warnock	94
6	Austin's Distinction between Locutionary and Illocutionary Acts	100
	Appendix: Austin's Use of the Word 'Meaning' and its Cognates in *How to do Things with Words*	115
	Bibliography of Published Philosophical and Related Works of R. M. Hare	117

Editor's Foreword

Professor Hare is the foremost exponent of the ethical theory known as prescriptivism. This theory of the logical character of moral speech-acts finds definitive expression in Hare's two books *The Language of Morals* (1952) and *Freedom and Reason* (1963). These books have aroused the interest of all modern moral philosophers and, by action or reaction, have been amongst the most influential of contemporary writings on ethics. In the present volume and the three other collections of Hare's papers which appear in this series some matters dealt with in Hare's books receive fuller consideration and some matters not treated there are discussed.

Probably the most interesting controversy in modern moral philosophy is that between those who believe Hare's views to be in the main right and those who have reacted fiercely against them and who are coming to be known as descriptivists. The present collection of papers, along with the other three, is an essential source for anyone who wishes to understand clearly and fully what is involved in prescriptivism *versus* descriptivism.

W. D. HUDSON

University of Exeter

Preface

The present volume is one of several in which I am collecting the more substantial of my published papers, together with some hitherto unpublished material on related topics. Apart from minor editorial corrections, the papers are printed as they first appeared, although I might now express myself differently. In making these papers more accessible, I hope that I may serve the convenience of those who share with me an interest in these fields; and with the same purpose I have added to this volume a bibliography, as complete and accurate as I could make it, of all that I have published in philosophy. I am grateful to the original publishers of the papers now reprinted for giving their permission where necessary; details of first publication will be found in the bibliography under the year appearing after the title of the essays in the table of contents. I am also most grateful to the General Editor of the series, and to its publishers, for their help and encouragement.

R. M. HARE

Corpus Christi College
Oxford
1971

Acknowledgements

Mind, LVIII (1949), LXXVI (1967); *Proceedings of the University of Western Ontario Colloquium,* ed. R. Binkley (1971); *Fetsckrift til Alf Ross,* ed. V. Kruse (1969); *Philosophical Review,* LXXIX (1970).

I   Imperative Sentences

It has often been taken for granted by logicians that there is a class of sentences which is the proper subject-matter of logic, and that they are at liberty to ignore all sentences which are not included in this class. For example, most logicians would undertake to tell you something about the sentence 'It is raining'; for instance, that it contradicted the sentence 'It is not raining'; but if confronted with the sentence 'What a foul day it is!' they would be likely to look down their noses and refuse to say anything about the logic of such a sentence. This would seem a natural attitude to adopt. But it is much more difficult to say precisely what are the criteria which determine whether or not a sentence is to be admitted into the logical fold. This article is an attempt to cast doubt upon one such criterion which has been popular recently, and in so doing to shed some light on the question, 'What is Logic about?'

The criterion which I shall be attacking has been formulated in various ways, but more often taken for granted without being formulated at all. The sort of sentences which are to be admitted into the logical fold are variously referred to as 'scientific', 'cognitive', 'informative', 'fact-stating', 'true-or-false', 'theoretical', 'referential', 'symbolic', etc.; and the sort of sentences which are to be excluded are called 'emotive', 'evocative', 'non-fact-stating', etc. The latter are held not to state genuine propositions, and therefore, since propositions are the bricks out of which a logical system is built, to be altogether beyond the pale of such a system. They are sometimes even said to be 'literally senseless'.

As examples of the view which I am attacking, the following passages may be quoted:

> In the scientific use of language ... the connexions and relations of references to one another must be of the kind which we call logical. ... But, for emotive purposes logical

First published in *Mind*, LVIII (1949).

arrangement is not necessary. (I. A. Richards, *Principles of Literary Criticism*, p. 268)

The symbolic use of words is *statement*; the recording, the support, the organisation and the communication of references. The emotive use of words is . . . the use of words to express or excite feelings and attitudes. . . .

The best test of whether our use of words is essentially symbolic or emotive is the question 'Is this true or false in the ordinary scientific sense?' If this question is relevant then the use is symbolic, if it is clearly irrelevant then we have an emotive utterance. (C. K. Ogden and I. A. Richards, *Meaning of Meaning*, pp. 149 f.)

When language is used simply in order to refer to a referend, its use is *scientific*. When it is used in order to arouse an emotional attitude in the hearer, to influence him in any way other than by giving him information, then its use is *emotive*. . . .

What is called logical connexion has little relevance to the emotive use of language, whereas it is the condition of success in scientific language. (L. S. Stebbing, *Modern Introduction to Logic*, pp. 17 f.)

The word 'meaning' is here always understood in the sense of 'designative meaning', sometimes also called 'cognitive', 'theoretical', 'referential', or 'informative', as distinguished from other meaning components, e.g. emotive or motivative meaning. Thus here we have to do only with declarative sentences and their parts. (R. Carnap, *Meaning and Necessity*, p. 6)

We may perhaps give this criterion sufficient precision for our purposes by saying that it excludes from the subject-matter of logic all sentences except those which purport to give information, i.e. to state that something is or is not the case. Because sentences which do this are properly put in the indicative mood, I shall refer to them henceforth as 'indicative sentences'. The term has the advantage of being, as yet, emotively neutral. The criterion which I am attacking says, then, that indicative sentences are the only sentences with which logic is called upon to deal.

The way in which I shall attack it is as follows. I shall take a class of sentences, namely imperatives, which clearly do not purport to state that anything is the case, and shall show that their logical behaviour is in many respects as exemplary as that of indicative sentences, and in particular that it is possible to infer an imperative conclusion from imperative premisses. I hope by this means to show that logicians have been wrong to confine their attention to indicative sentences.

In thus refusing to confine logical enquiry to sentences which state that something is the case, I shall be following a suggestion of Professor G. Ryle's, who has rightly warned us (*Ar. Soc.* 1945–6) not to imagine that all knowledge is knowledge *that* something is the case, but to realise that there is another important kind of knowledge, knowledge *how* to do something. Knowledge that something is the case is normally communicated by means of indicative sentences. Knowledge how to do something is normally communicated, where it can be communicated at all, by means of imperative sentences, as can be seen by looking at any cookery-book. If, therefore, logic is to tell us anything about this second sort of knowledge, it will have to enquire into the behaviour of imperative as well as indicative sentences.

There is another reason which makes such an enquiry urgent. The imperative mood has in recent years been in danger of being used as a dumping ground for sentences which have failed to establish their *bona fides* as propositions, usually because they cannot be said to be either true or false. The most important class of sentences which have been classed with imperatives for this reason is that of ethical sentences. The notion that these are crypto-imperatives, or contain an imperative element, has been suggested by R. Carnap (*Philosophy and Logical Syntax*, p. 23), who regards this as a reason for banishing ethics from philosophy; and by C. D. Broad (*Ar. Soc.* 1933–4); and the idea has been developed in greater detail by C. L. Stevenson (*Ethics and Language*, pp. 21 ff.). Most of the writers who take this view of ethics seem to subscribe to the criterion which I am attacking; for they seem, unlike Kant, to class imperative sentences with emotive utterances, and to think that, because ethical sentences are not true indicatives, logical methods cannot be used in ethics with as much confidence as in other enquiries. A sentence that does not state that something is the case is at once suspect.

Now it is an important discovery, if true, that ethical sentences do not tell us that something is the case; but the right thing to do after making such a discovery is to ask what they do tell us, and how to frame them so that this telling is done without ambiguities and contradictions; in fact, to find out what are the logical rules for talking ethically. It may be that there are no such rules; but this does not follow from the premiss – although that may also be true – that ethical sentences do not state that something is the case. That philosophers have been led to abandon ethics to the psychologists, just because ethical sentences are not fact-stating, shows how firmly established has become the criterion of logicality which I am attacking.

Ethical sentences are not the only kind of sentences to be suspected of being imperatives in disguise. They are in good company. Some have said that definitions, and some even that all analytical sentences, are rules; and a rule is a universal imperative. Rules of inference, too, are prominent in modern logic-books; and the list could be added to. It is true that rules have been discussed a lot recently; but perhaps we shall not discover much more about rules, or universal imperatives, until we enquire more closely into the behaviour of imperative sentences in general. Such an enquiry would most naturally begin with simple singular commands like 'Come in', and proceed later to more complicated sentences. To do otherwise would be like starting a logic textbook with a chapter on universal sentences.

These and other reasons make an enquiry into the logical behaviour of imperative sentences urgent. As a prolegomenon to such an enquiry, I propose, in this article, first to draw attention to some features of the grammar of imperatives in ordinary speech, and then to exhibit some logical characteristics of the imperative mood. I shall start by separating from the rest of language that part of it which consists of sentences. This means that I shall say nothing about what are usually called exclamations or interjections, nor about collections of words, such as subordinate clauses, which can form parts of sentences, but cannot be sentences in themselves. Now sentences are traditionally divided into three classes, statements, commands and questions. Of these three sorts of sentence, the last, the question, although it has assumed great importance in the thought of some philosophers, for example Cook Wilson and Collingwood, seems not to be so basic as the other two. It would seem, in fact, that questions can be translated without loss of meaning into commands; thus 'Who is at the door?'

can be translated 'Name the person who is at the door' (where 'who' is of course a relative and not an indirect interrogative), and 'Are you married?' can be translated

> I am/am not* married.
> *Strike out whichever is inapplicable.

Here again, 'whichever' is of course a relative. In general, a question can be translated into a command, either to put values to the variables in a sentential function, or to assert one of the component sentences of a disjunction.

Apart, therefore, from noticing that we have here another addition to the list of crypto-imperatives, we need say no more about questions. We are left, according to the traditional division, with indicatives and imperatives. As we shall see, the traditional division is faulty in that it lumps with imperatives a class of sentences, namely wishes, whose function is quite different from that of true imperatives; but for the moment it will be instructive to compare the behaviour of the two main groups, indicatives and imperatives.

The first and most obvious grammatical difference between the two moods is that the imperative mood occupies in the pages of most grammar-books very much less space than the indicative. This is because the imperative is defective in many parts. Let us see which these parts are. In the first place, certain *tenses* do not have any imperatives at all. For reasons which, though obvious, are of interest, we do not command things to happen in the past. Secondly, even in those tenses which have imperatives, all the *persons* are seldom represented. I suppose that all languages have second persons singular and plural in the imperative mood; the second person seems, indeed, to be the person for which this mood has the greatest liking; and again, it will be instructive to enquire why this is so. But we also find, as in Greek, third persons singular and plural, or, as in French, first persons plural. Hindustani has something very like a first-person singular imperative, which means, by courteous implication, 'Please command me to . . .'. These forms, however, we feel to be oddities. Why is it, then, that commands are normally given in the second person and in the present or future tense?

We may, I think, take a hint here from Aristotle's very important discussion of deliberation and choice in *Eth. Nic.* III, where he is discussing in psychological terms very much the same problem as we are here discussing in linguistic terms.[1] Put most generally, the reason for the restrictions on the scope of the imperative mood which we have noticed is that it is concerned only with states of affairs which are brought about by human action. An indicative sentence is an answer to the question 'What is the case?'; an imperative sentence is an answer to the question 'What is to be the case?' or 'What am I to make the case?' The first question presupposes that there is some unalterable fact to be stated; the second question, on the contrary, presupposes that there is a choice between alternative facts, i.e. between alternative courses of action. To ask the second sort of question is to deliberate; to answer it is either to choose, if the question was asked about our own action, or to command, if it was asked about someone else's. We should neither deliberate, nor choose, nor command, unless it were in question whether the action were going to be performed or not. But this is never the case with past actions; therefore there are no true past imperatives.

The reason for the preponderance of the second person in imperative sentences is similar. Since a command can only be carried out by someone doing something, it is natural to address it to that person, and tell him to do whatever it is. But there are cases in which it is inappropriate or impossible to speak thus; hence the existence of other persons of the mood.

It is possible, however, for logical purposes, to adopt a language in which neither of these restrictions as to tense and person apply to the imperative mood. The tense-restriction can be eliminated as follows. Instead of giving our time-indications by tenses of verbs, we give them by reference to some fixed era; for example, the birth of Christ. This means that an event whose time would be given, in tense-notation, by verbs in the past, present or future tenses, according to the date of utterance of the sentence, will be given instead, univocally, by means of a date. Thus, for any imaginable event, it is possible to imagine an imperative sentence which commands that event to take place; we do not need to specify when the sentence was uttered, since the date of the event referred to has been already given. The sentence is one which might have been uttered at any time

[1] 1112 a18 ff. In reprinting this paragraph I have omitted some allusions to the Greek text.

previous to the event referred to; whether it was uttered or not is a matter of contingent fact which does not concern the logician. In this way, for any indicative sentence describing an event, we can frame a corresponding imperative sentence commanding that event to happen. Of course, the command may be physically impossible of fulfilment; but this again is a matter of contingent fact.

The restriction as to person, which is in any case much less hard and fast, could be removed entirely if circumstances so required. We do not in fact use the first person singular, because we do not need to tell ourselves to do things, we just do them. If we were so constituted that we could not act without first giving ourselves an order, we should have a first-person imperative; in fact, we already have a form of speech for those exceptional circumstances in which we do tell ourselves to do things; we say 'Let me think'; 'Let me see', etc. On the other hand, if we were omnipotent, and could command the obedience of all persons and all things, we should no doubt make great use of third-person imperatives (cf. Genesis i. 3). Given such omnipotence, anything could become the subject of a command; any event which could be described by an indicative sentence could equally well be commanded by an imperative sentence. The two moods would then be co-extensive, and there would be a one-one correspondence between statements and commands. That this is not so in our ordinary grammar is merely a sign that we are not omnipotent; and this again is a contingent fact which does not concern the logician. I shall therefore assume that a logician is entitled to construct imperatives in all persons and in all tenses.

We may now state with greater precision what is the difference between indicative and imperative sentences as regards their relation to fact. An indicative sentence tells us that something is the case. An imperative sentence tells us to make something the case. Let us compare the following two sentences:

(1) Mary, please show Mrs Prendergast her room.
(2) Mary will show you your room, Mrs Prendergast.

Both these sentences refer to something which might be the case, and would be the case if Mary were to conduct Mrs Prendergast upstairs, open the door, etc. We may call this something

Showing of her room to Mrs Prendergast by Mary at time t (where t is shortly after the sentences are uttered). These words are not a sentence. They are the description of a complex series of events; but they are not a sentence because there is something missing; to be complete, they would have either to say that the events described happened or would happen, or to command them to happen, or to ask whether they were going to happen, or something else of this general nature.

It is now necessary, for the sake of compactness, to introduce some technical terms. We have seen that part of what both the above sentences do is to describe a series of events – the same events in both cases – which we called 'Showing of her room to Mrs Prendergast by Mary at time t'. I shall call this part of what a sentence does its 'descriptive' function. As we shall see, it is always possible, at the cost of artificiality, to frame a sentence in such a way that the words which perform this descriptive function are separable from the words which do the other things which a sentence has to do. I shall call the part of the sentence which performs the descriptive function of that sentence its 'descriptor'. In sentences (1) and (2) above, the descriptor is not explicit. It can be made explicit as follows: let us write, instead of sentence (1)

(1.1) Showing of her room to Mrs Prendergast by Mary at time t, please.

and instead of sentence (2)

(2.1) Showing of her room to Mrs Prendergast by Mary at time t, yes.

We are to understand (1) and (1.1) as having the same meaning, and likewise (2) and (2.1). It is hardly necessary to point out that the contradictory of (2.1), according to the usage which I am suggesting, is not

Showing of her room to Mrs Prendergast by Mary at time t, no,

but

No showing of her room to Mrs Prendergast by Mary at time t, yes.

That is to say, negatives go into the descriptor. 'Yes' and

'please' in the above sentences do nothing but indicate the mood of the sentence, whether indicative or imperative or whatever it is. We need a generic name for the function which these words perform; and I shall call it the 'dictive' function, because it is they that really do the *saying* (the commanding, stating, etc.) which a sentence does. The descriptor, on the other hand, describes what it is that is being said. I shall call that part of a sentence which performs the dictive function, the 'dictor'. Dictors, like descriptors, can be either implicit or explicit.

In English, as in most languages, dictors and descriptors are implicit; they cannot be separated without artificially recasting sentences. Even in English, however, we can say of a sentence what mood it is in; there must, therefore, be something about it which tells us this. This, then, is the dictor, and the rest is the descriptor. For example, we know that the sentence 'Come in' is a command because it lacks a personal pronoun, and this absence of a pronoun is, in an Irish sense, a symbol for the imperative dictor. In Latin, we know that 'Intrate' is an imperative because of its termination; and so the termination contains the dictor; but of course it also contains something else which belongs to the descriptor, not the dictor, namely the indication of person. There may be no languages in which dictors and descriptors are completely explicit; but for logical purposes we shall have to make them so artificially.

Against the words 'dictive' and 'dictor' I hope there will be no objection. But it may be said that I have misused the word 'descriptive'. It is true that this word has been much used recently as a term of approval for what I have here been calling indicative sentences – those, that is to say, which state that something is the case. The people who use it thus are generally those who adopt the criterion of logicality among sentences which I am attacking. Their usage is not, it would seem, in accord with common practice; for the word 'describe' is often used in connexion with commands; we say 'Will you please describe more precisely what you are telling me to do', or 'I described to him in the minutest detail how to find the house' (which means, for example, that I said to him, 'Go down the road and take the second turning to the right, etc.'). I therefore make no apology for following the common usage and saying that imperatives 'describe' a course of action which is to be taken.

I shall call that which is described by the descriptor, the 'descriptum'. The descriptum of an indicative sentence is what would be the case if the sentence were true; and of an imperative sentence, what would be the case if it were obeyed. The descriptum of a statement may or may not be actually a fact; if the sentence is true, it is; if not, not. The descriptum of a command may or may not become a fact; if the command is obeyed, it does; if not, not. As the verificationists have pointed out, one of the ways in which a statement can be meaningless is by having no descriptum, i.e. nothing that would be the case if it were true, or that would verify it. An imperative sentence can be meaningless in the same way. The sentence 'Sing me a rope of exuberant soap' is for me 'descriptively' meaningless, because I do not know what action it describes and tells me to do.

We must therefore admit the value of much that has been said by verificationists; there is such a thing as descriptive meaning, and a sentence must have it, if it is to be used for certain purposes, such as the conveying of information or orders. But to say this is not to say that sentences which are not true-or-false are meaningless, even descriptively; for other sentences than indicatives may have descriptive meaning, in the sense in which we are now using that word.

The distinction which we have made between descriptors and dictors enables us to state concisely what is the relation of an imperative sentence to the corresponding indicative sentence. The two sentences have the same descriptor, but different dictors; in other words, what one states to be the case, the other commands to be the case. The difference between the two sentences is confined to the dictor. If, therefore, we want to tell, in any sentence, which symbols are dictive and which descriptive, all we have to do is to frame the corresponding imperative or indicative, as the case may be, and see wherein it differs from the original sentence. The difference will be in the dictor; the resemblance will be in the descriptor. The process is easier if we use the type of artificial translation which I have suggested; but it can in principle be performed with any imperative or indicative sentence. We shall see, if we try out this method on sentences containing logical connectives, that these connectives are all descriptive and not dictive. In fact, it is the descriptive part of sentences with which formal logicians are almost exclusively concerned; and this means that what they say applies as much to imperatives as to indicatives; for to any descriptor we can add either kind of dictor, and get a sentence.

This point has been put in another way by saying that imperative sentences 'contain an indicative factor' (J. Jörgensen, *Erkenntnis*, VII, 291). This is perhaps misleading. They do indeed contain a factor (the descriptor) which is also contained in statements; but they do not contain the specifically 'indicative factor' of statements, viz. their indicative dictor. This misleading form of expression has led some people to talk as if an imperative inference, such as those we shall consider, were really, as it were, an indicative inference in disguise; and it might be argued on this basis that imperatives are not logical as such, but only in virtue of their indicative factor. Granted this interpretation of 'indicative factor' to mean what we have called 'descriptor', such a contention is sound; but it would be equally sound to call the descriptor of indicative sentences an 'imperative factor', and so to argue that indicatives were not logical as such, but only in virtue of their 'imperative factor'. A less misleading form of expression is to say that there is a factor, the descriptor, which is contained in both indicatives and imperatives, and that it is this descriptor that we operate with in most, if not all, logical inferences.

In order to illustrate this, and to make quite clear the distinction between descriptors and dictors, I shall give some more examples. The first in each pair is the English sentence; the second is its translation, making the dictor and descriptor explicit.

(3) Do not walk on the grass.
(3.1) No walking on the grass (by anyone ever), please.
(4) Nobody ever walks on the grass.
(4.1) No walking on the grass by anyone ever, yes.
(5) If the train has not gone, catch it.
(5.1) In event of train not being gone, catching of it by you, please.
(6) If the train has not gone, you will catch it.
(6.1) In event of train not being gone, catching of it by you, yes.
(7) Go and see.

(7.1) Going and seeing by you, please.
(8) Talk sense or get out.
(8.1) Talking sense by you or getting out by you, please.

Let us now go further, and see what happens to these descriptors and dictors when we perform an inference. Consider the following disjunctive syllogism:

> You will use an axe or a saw.
> You will not use an axe.
> ―――――――――――――――
> You will use a saw.

Let us translate it as before,

> Use of axe or saw by you shortly, yes.
> No use of axe by you shortly, yes.
> ―――――――――――――――
> Use of saw by you shortly, yes.

Now let us put all these sentences into the imperative. Suppose I say to someone, 'Use an axe or a saw', and then, fearing that he may cut off his leg, say 'No, don't use an axe'. He will, without further instruction, infer that he is to use a saw. This syllogism, translated, becomes,

> Use of axe or saw by you shortly, please.
> No use of axe by you shortly, please.
> ―――――――――――――――
> Use of saw by you shortly, please.

We notice that in these two syllogisms, one indicative and one imperative, the descriptors are the same; only the dictors are different. This is as we should expect; for it is only in the dictor that an imperative differs from the corresponding indicative. We also notice that the dictors seem not to make any difference to the argument. We could write:

> Use of axe or saw by you shortly.
> No use of axe by you shortly.
> ―――――――――――――――
> Use of saw by you shortly.

If the premisses describe a situation, then the conclusion also describes that situation, though not necessarily so fully as the premisses do. We can then add whichever set of dictors we please. If we command someone to use an axe or a saw, and then not to use an axe, we command him to use a saw; if we say that he will use an axe or a saw, and then that he will not use an axe, we say that he will use a saw.

We may put this more formally as follows. Let C be a command, and let S be a statement with the same descriptor. Let $c_1, c_2, \ldots, c_n$ be commands which can be inferred from C (i.e. whose descriptors describe states of affairs which logically must be the case if the state of affairs described by the descriptor of C is the case); and analogously for S and $s_1, s_2, \ldots, s_n$. Then if we command C we command $c_1, c_2, \ldots, c_n$; that is to say, if we command to be the case what is described by the descriptor of C, we command to be the case what is described by the descriptors of $c_1, c_2, \ldots, c_n$. Since this assertion, if misunderstood, can give rise to paradox, it requires further explanation. It does not, in the first place, follow that to obey c_1, for example, is to obey C, any more than that to verify s_1, a logical consequence of S, is to verify S; in either case to claim this would be to make an improper conversion. We cannot therefore, if given a command, or set of commands, deduce one or more consequences of those commands, and think that if we have obeyed the latter we have done all that was commanded by the former. For example, if C was 'Put on your parachute and jump out', and we inferred the consequential command 'Jump out', and obeyed this, we should be only partially fulfilling the command given, in this case with disastrous consequences. There are other examples even more paradoxical, in which to fulfil a consequential command is not to fulfil the original command at all; and these have led some people to suppose that the logic of imperative sentences is radically different from the logic of indicatives. The point has been clarified to a certain extent by A. Ross in an illuminating article, 'Imperatives and Logic' (*Phil. of Science*, XI (1944) 41). Consider the following example of Ross's. An indicative inference of the form

$$\frac{\text{You will post the letter}}{\text{You will burn or post the letter}}$$

is valid in ordinary logic, but the corresponding imperative inference

$$\frac{\text{Post the letter}}{\text{Burn or post the letter}}$$

appears to us paradoxical, because we think it means that if we told someone to post a letter, he might make this inference and so think he would do what he was told if he obeyed the conclusion by burning the letter. The reasons for the paradox are worth examining. First, but of minor importance, is the fact that the inference, like the corresponding indicative one, is trivial, and therefore would never be made. The second reason is the one which we have already suggested. Let C be the command 'Post the letter' and c_1 be the command 'Burn or post the letter'. When I said above that to command C is to command c_1 I did not mean that to obey c_1 was to obey C. Let us imagine that a stupid but logical person is told to post a letter. Let us suppose that he is stupid enough not to know that if he burns it he can't also post it. What can he infer from the command? He cannot infer that burning the letter would break the command, because for all he knows he can burn it *and* post it. He does, however, know that if he *breaks* the command c_1 (which he can only do by neither posting nor burning it) then he breaks the original command C. This inference is the imperative equivalent of the indicative inference

$$\frac{S \text{ entails } s_1}{\text{Not-}s_1 \text{ entails not-}S}$$

He also knows that he must not break any other command which follows from C. Suppose he then discovers that burning the letter rules out the possibility of posting it. He then knows that he must not burn it; for if he did, he could not post it. It is the fact that we assume everyone to possess this latter piece of knowledge which, among other reasons, makes this imperative inference appear paradoxical, though it is in fact valid.

It appears, then, that it is possible, by reasoning in imperatives, to guide our actions. We cannot indeed, when given a command, infer other commands from it, and think that by fulfilling them we have fulfilled the original command, and done all that we were told to do; but we can infer that unless we fulfil at least the deduced commands we have *not* done all that we were told to do. Thus imperative inferences may be of use from the point of view of the person commanded. From the point of view of the person commanding they may also be of use. He knows that if he commands C he also commands $c_1, c_2, \ldots, c_n$; that is to say, he makes himself responsible, as it were, for the logical consequences of his command as well as the command itself; and this may be of use in helping him to decide what to command.

The method of reasoning used in such inferences is, of course, exactly that which is used in indicative logic; these considerations in no way support the theory that there can be a separate 'Logic of Imperatives', but only that imperatives *are* logical in the same way as indicatives. This is because both imperatives and indicatives contain descriptors, which are the parts of sentences which we normally operate with in our reasoning. Thus most inferences are inferences from descriptor to descriptor, and we could add whichever set of dictors we pleased.

It is even possible to mix dictors within the same syllogism; Aristotle does it in his practical syllogism, where the major is usually a universal imperative, the minor an indicative, and the conclusion either a further imperative, or an action which, so to speak, elides an imperative. But since I have not yet investigated the rules which make such mixed syllogisms valid or invalid, I shall not deal with them here.

In case it should still be doubted whether it is possible to argue in imperatives, here is another example:

> When you come to the cross-roads, turn right.
> Before you turn right, give the appropriate signal.
> ―――――――――――――――――――――――――
> Before you come to the cross-roads, give the appropriate signal.

In this case, as in (6) above, it might be asked whether there are indicative dictors concealed in the subordinate clauses. That this is not so can be seen by translating in the usual manner:

> On coming to the cross-roads turning right by you, please.
> Before turning right giving of appropriate signal by you, please.
> ―――――――――――――――――――――――――
> Before coming to the cross-roads giving of appropriate signal by you, please.

Only main verbs contain dictors.

Closely connected with the fact that it is possible to infer in imperatives, is the fact that it is possible to contradict oneself in them. As all soldiers know, it is possible to give or receive contradictory orders. An example would be 'Advance to the left . . .'; a squad can either move to the left, or advance, but not both. Another would be, 'No. 1 (gun), five rounds, troop fire'; troop fire is, by definition, fired by more than one gun. For the purposes of discussion, I shall take a more elementary example, which would never in fact occur, 'Both do and do not do *X*'. This command is self-contradictory in the same way as the corresponding indicative sentence 'You will both do and not do *X*'. The same self-contradiction occurs in both these two sentences, because both their descriptors are the same, and self-contradictory. The descriptor is 'Doing of *X* by you shortly and not doing of *X* by you shortly'. Whichever dictor we add to this, the result is a self-contradiction.

That it is descriptors and not dictors which contradict, will appear also from the following consideration. To contradict, we have, if we make ourselves explicit, to use the symbol of negation. This, as we have seen, belongs to the descriptor, like the other chief logical signs. It belongs to the descriptor, because it has nothing to do with the mood of a sentence. It will follow a sentence in all its moods.

It would appear, then, that inference and contradiction, two of the things about sentences which logic especially studies, can be studied in commands as well as in statements. This is because these processes are to be found in the descriptive part of sentences, which is common to both moods. We may go further, and assert that any formula of formal logic which is capable of an indicative interpretation is capable also of an imperative one. The proof is as follows. Let S be any formula which is a complete sentence, and which has an indicative interpretation. This means that there is something which it states to be the case. This, in our terminology, means that it has a descriptor and an indicative dictor. Now if any state of affairs (whether actual or not) is described by the descriptor of this sentence, it must be possible, instead of stating this state of affairs to be the case, to command it to be the case; i.e. we can substitute for the indicative dictor an imperative one, leaving the descriptor unchanged. This leaves us with an imperative sentence which is as much an interpretation of the original formula as the indicative one.

Let us take as established this principle, that any sentence-formula which is capable of an indicative interpretation is capable also of an imperative one; and let us imagine it applied to all the sentences in a logic-book. We shall call it 'The principle of the dictive indifference of logic'. We shall see that it applies to what are called 'object-sentences' but not to what are called 'meta-sentences'. All the logical characteristics of object-sentences will remain the same in either interpretation, because they will contain the same descriptors, i.e. the same logical connectives and the same expressions connected by them; and this is all that logical formulae need to contain, in order to be used as object-sentences. For example, let us suppose that a logician quotes the familiar syllogism which begins 'All men are mortal'. This syllogism could be rewritten:

> Let all men be mortal.
> Let Socrates be a man.
> ———————————
> Let Socrates be mortal.

and would remain valid, for the reason that its descriptors, which are the same as those in the indicative syllogism, form a valid inference:

> All men mortal:
> Socrates man:
> ———————————
> Socrates mortal:

Similarly, all arguments which are conducted in object-sentences will remain valid in the new interpretation. But the dictive indifference of object-sentences is not shared by meta-sentences which a logician uses to *say* things about his object-sentences. For example, suppose that, after quoting the above syllogism, he goes on, 'This is a syllogism, and all syllogisms of this form are valid', we could not, without altering his meaning, rewrite the remark as 'Let this be a syllogism, and let all syllogisms of this form be valid'. He wants to *state* that it *is* a syllogism and that they *are* valid; and he can only do this by making a statement, i.e. by using an indicative dictor.

The reason for this distinction between object-sentences and meta-sentences in respect of their dictive indifference should be obvious. When a logician writes down an object-sentence, he is mentioning it and not using it; that is to say, he is not *saying* whatever the sentence is designed to say, but only quoting it as an example of something that someone might say. He does this in order to examine the logical properties of the sentence; and as these are all logical properties of the descriptor, he could, if he wished, ignore the dictor; in fact, he could treat his object-formulae just as descriptors. But when he uses a meta-sentence to *say* something about an object-sentence, he really is saying something; and to say something, he has to use a dictor; otherwise we should not know whether he was commanding or stating or asking or something else.

There is one respect, however, in which an imperative interpretation of the object-sentences in a logic-book would necessitate a radical recasting of the meta-linguistic part of the book. Most logic-books are written on the assumption that the formulae mentioned in them are to be interpreted indicatively. They therefore, in their meta-linguistic remarks, use forms of expression which are not appropriate to imperative object-sentences. For example, they use the words 'true' and 'false' of the object-sentences; and imperative sentences are not either true or false. I should like to suggest that the use of the words 'true' and 'false' in logic-books is often a blemish, and that this blemish would be removed if the meta-sentences were recast in order to accommodate an imperative interpretation of the object-sentences. Logic is primarily concerned, not with the truth of propositions, but with the validity of inferences; and it has long been a commonplace of traditional logic that it makes no difference to the validity of an inference whether its premisses and conclusion are true or whether they are false. The argument is valid if the conclusion follows from the premisses, whether true or false, or, we may add, neither. It is true that we often say that *if* the premisses are true, then the conclusion is true. But this is a concession to the indicative mood which we need not make. In our terminology, we could ignore the dictors, and say that *if* the descriptors of the premisses describe a state of affairs, then the conclusion describes, at least partially, the same state of affairs. Whether the state of affairs is actually the case makes no difference to the validity of the argument. References to truth and falsehood are therefore irrelevant.

There is no room here to attempt a detailed recasting of the terminology of logicians to accommodate imperative sentences. I am satisfied that such devices as truth-tables can be so modified without impairing their performance of their function. Other uses of the words 'true' and 'false', especially in semantical discussions, will create more difficulties. In particular, definitions of validity in terms of truth will need careful examination. But to discuss these difficulties would carry me outside the scope of this article, which is in any case intended only as a first reconnaissance of the subject. Let us rather repeat our main conclusion, that since logic is mainly about descriptors, and commands contain descriptors, commands are a proper concern of the logician.

There is one objection that might be made to this contention. It might be said that, although commands contain words which in statements would be called logical words, and although they behave in a manner which superficially resembles that of statements, they are unreliable from the logical point of view, because their real function is motivative, emotive, hortative, evocative, etc., that is to say, their object is to produce emotions in the hearer, especially such emotions as lead to actions; and emotions are best kept out of logic. Such an objection would naturally be made by an upholder of the view that I am attacking, that it is only true-or-false fact-stating indicative sentences which can safely be discussed by the logician. Confronted with any sentence which is not true-or-false, which claims to state no fact, one who holds such a view finds it hard to ascribe to the sentence any kind of meaning which is logically reputable; he therefore has to find some other sort of meaning to ascribe to it; and emotive meaning is a possible candidate. It is not a very plausible one in the case of imperatives; for they, after all, include laws, about which counsel are supposed to produce logical and dispassionate arguments, and rules of inference, which are the bases of logical systems themselves. But nevertheless, let us see whether commands are more emotive than other kinds of sentence.

There are in general two ways in which a sentence may be emotive. It may express emotions which are affecting the speaker; or it may evoke emotions in the hearer. In the former case, I shall say that the sentence is expressive, in the latter, evocative. A sentence may well do both these things; it may also have emotive meaning in addition to other sorts of meaning, for example, descriptive meaning and dictive meaning. Since emotive meaning is exhaustively divided into expressive and evocative meaning, we must enquire whether commands possess either of these two sorts of meaning in a greater degree than, for example, statements.

Since the sort of emotion that a command would be most naturally said to express is a wish or desire that something should take place, it will be instructive to compare commands with another sort of sentence that somewhat resembles them, wish-sentences. Now it is at least plausible to maintain that when David said 'Would God I had died for thee, O Absalom, my son, my son', he was not trying to give information, either about himself or about his son, but was expressing an emotion, namely the wish that he had died. Note that even this highly emotive utterance has some descriptive meaning, in the sense in which we have been using the term; David had to know what would have been the case if the wish had been fulfilled, i.e. that he himself would have been dead and Absalom alive. But the sentence is nevertheless charged with emotion, and we should be unwise to examine its logic too closely. Contrast this sentence with a dull command like 'Come in'. This does not mean in the least the same as 'Would God you would come in'. 'Come in' may, indeed, express emotion in two senses. In the weak sense, it expresses a wish, not like David's utterance, but in the same sort of way as an indicative sentence expresses a *belief* that something is the case. In the strong sense, the words 'Come in' may, by the tone in which they are uttered, express emotion, in the sense of agitation or some other powerful feeling. For example, if I think that the man outside the door is an assassin, my words may express apprehension; on the other hand, if I think that he is an old friend, they may express welcome. But in this sense, any sentence whatever may express emotion; Professor Ryle gives the example of 'Seven sevens are forty-nine' said by an angry schoolmaster to a stupid schoolboy who had made a mistake. It may even be true, as Collingwood and others have thought, that all language is in origin and by nature expressive; certainly it would seem that any sentence which is actually used must at least express an interest in its subject; else why should it be said ? At any rate there is no reason to suppose that commands are more expressive than statements in any sense. How expressive a sentence is, can hardly ever be decided by looking at the mere words of which it is composed, let alone by simply noticing what mood it is in. It depends on the circumstances, the context, the tone of voice, and many other factors.

If commands are not markedly more expressive than other sentences, are they more evocative ? Here again, we must be careful to distinguish between different ways in which a sentence may evoke, or be designed to evoke, emotion. In the strong sense, 'emotion' may mean 'agitation or some other violent state of feeling'. In this sense, any sentence may be evocative; for example, the statement 'A scorpion has just crawled up your trouser-leg' might be highly evocative, and the command 'Come in' highly unevocative. In the weak sense, a sentence might be said to be evocative if it is intended to, or does, produce *any* change in the hearer's state of mind or behaviour. In this sense it would be hard to find any sentence that was not evocative. At the least, a sentence that is heard and understood must produce the dispositional property called 'understanding the sentence'. It is true that commands are designed to produce an action, or a will to action, in the hearer; but even this does not necessarily make them more evocative than other sentences. If you want a man to take off his trousers, you will more readily succeed by saying 'A scorpion has just crawled up your trouser-leg' than by saying 'Take off your trousers'.

It is, in short, impossible to ascribe the logically undesirable character of emotivity to classes of sentences *en bloc*. It is quite true that the logician should be on his guard against the danger of trying to be more logical about any group of words than its nature will bear; but this does not absolve him from doing his job, which is to tell us how to say whatever we want to say without ambiguity or inconsistency. If there is any kind of sentence in which precision and consistency are virtues, then it is the logician's business to tell us how to achieve them. If commands are such a kind of sentence, then the logician must study the imperative mood.[1]

[1] I have included the above paper, not simply for sentimental reasons as my first-published article, but because it contains insights which I still think important. It also contains a number of errors, most of which are corrected in the succeeding papers. The following Appendix is printed in order to remedy the mistake I made of omitting the passage when revising the thesis to form the first part of *The Language of Morals* (see p. 90 of this volume).

Appendix

Extract from 'Practical Reason', an unpublished thesis awarded the T. H. Green Prize at Oxford, 1950.

[The] dictor has an obvious affinity with the so-called 'assertion-sign' of Frege, and with the similar sign of Russell and Whitehead. It is interesting to reflect on the fate of this symbol, which is not now much used by logicians. Russell and Whitehead introduce their assertion-sign as follows:

> The sign '⊢', called the 'assertion sign', means that what follows is asserted. It is required for distinguishing a complete proposition, which we assert, from any subordinate propositions contained in it but not asserted. In ordinary written language a sentence contained between full stops denotes an asserted proposition, and if it is false, the book is in error. The sign '⊢' prefixed to a proposition serves this same purpose in our symbolism. For example, if '⊢ $(p \supset p)$' occurs, it is to be taken as a complete assertion convicting the authors of error unless the proposition '$p \supset p$' is true (as it is). Also a proposition stated in symbols without this sign '⊢' prefixed is not asserted, and is merely put forward for consideration, or as a subordinate part of an asserted proposition. (*Principia Mathematica*, 1, 9)

Now it seems to me that the sign '⊢' as so defined serves not one but three different purposes. These are:

(1) *A sign of completeness*. This is the function performed by a full stop in ordinary written language, and is referred to by the following words in the above definition (except those in brackets):

> ... required for distinguishing a complete proposition ... from any subordinate propositions contained in it ... it is to be taken as a complete [assertion]. ... Also a proposition stated in symbols without this sign '⊢' prefixed ... is ... a subordinate part of a ... proposition.

(2) *A sign of use.* This function is performed in ordinary written language by the absence of inverted commas round an expression; their presence indicates that the expression is being mentioned only, and not used. This function is referred to by the following words in the definition:

> ... means that what follows is asserted ... which we assert ... but not asserted ... if it is false, the book is in error ... convicting the authors of error unless the proposition '$p \supset p$' is true ... is not asserted, and is merely put forward for consideration.

That this function is not the same as (1) may easily be seen if we reflect that the subordinate parts of propositions (for example, conditional clauses) are just as much used as the whole sentences of which they form part. If we put them in inverted commas, the sense would be destroyed, and we should no longer be saying the same thing. For example, contrast the two following sentences:

> After line 537 of the *Agamemnon*, there is missing a line, if we are to believe Wilamowitz.
> After line 537 of the *Agamemnon*, there is missing a line, 'if we are to believe Wilamowitz'.

(3) *A sign of mood or dictor.* Russell's definition certainly implies that the assertion-sign performs a dictive function, though this is not made as explicit as the other two functions. Indeed, it follows from the performance of the other two functions that a dictive function must be understood; for unless a sentence has a dictor, it is not complete; and unless it is complete with a dictor, it cannot be used. The dictor understood is of course an indicative one. This is implied by the words:

> 'assertion-sign' ... is asserted ... which we assert ... but not asserted ... if it is false ... is true ...

It is fair to say, however, that Russell and Whitehead do not lay great stress on the necessity of this function being performed; they, like most other logicians, tacitly assume that all their sentences are in the indicative.

Thus the affinity of the dictor with Russell's assertion-sign is not very close.

It is interesting that Wittgenstein took the sign solely as a sign of use:

> Frege's assertion sign '⊢' is logically altogether meaningless; in Frege (and Russell) it only shows that these authors hold as true the propositions marked in this way. '⊢' belongs therefore to the proposition no more than does the number of the proposition. A proposition cannot possibly assert of itself that it is true. (*Tractatus* 4.442, trans. C. K. Ogden)

We have seen that the sign of use in ordinary written language is the absence of inverted commas (the sign of mention); and Wittgenstein – or his printer – like all careful logicians, uses this symbolism (which is indeed indispensable, if we are to mention sentences without using them). Thus Wittgenstein himself uses a symbol whose precise equivalent he condemns as 'logically altogether meaningless'. But in this he is not guilty of an inconsistency; for we are to realise, having read the *Tractatus*, that what he has been doing in the body of the work, namely talking about language – whence the necessity of inverted commas – was something which is in principle impossible; in a purified language inverted commas (at any rate the kind used in metalogic) would go the way of the rest of the *Tractatus*.

The reason for the disappearance of the symbol as a sign of use is that logicians, following the insistence of Carnap on this point, are now very careful in their use of inverted commas; thus the assertion-sign has had its place taken by an exact equivalent (in this function), the absence of inverted commas. The reason for its disappearance as a sign of completeness is that we can normally tell from its form whether a sentence is complete or not; if there is nothing missing to make it a complete sentence, we assume that it is one. It is, however, with its possible function as a dictor that we are here concerned. It may be doubted whether this function has ever been much stressed; so long as one is operating exclusively in the indicative mood, the need for dictors is not apparent. The assertion-sign does nevertheless perform by implication a dictive function, because as a result of Russell's definition no one could imagine that a sentence prefaced by it was in any mood but the indicative.

2 Some Alleged Differences between Imperatives and Indicatives

Anybody who studies imperative or deontic logic is bound to be very soon faced with the question of whether the logic or group of logics that he is studying differs radically from ordinary 'indicative' or 'assertoric' logic, or whether it can be accommodated, after a few relatively simple explanations, within the framework of ordinary logic. It would be foolish to pretend that this question can yet be settled. In this article I am going to maintain a less ambitious thesis: that several of the reasons which various writers have given for alleging differences between imperative and ordinary logic are based on misunderstandings. I shall divide these misunderstandings into two groups. The first can, I think, be removed by a straightforward application of Mr Grice's recent work on what he calls 'implicatures'; and the second, by insisting on the distinction, often ignored, between ordinary singular imperatives, on the one hand, and 'ought'-sentences on the other. This important distinction is obscured by those systems of deontic logic which use the same symbol or operator for both purposes.

As an example of the first group of alleged reasons for thinking that imperative logic must be different, consider the following inference:

Post the letter.
∴ Post the letter or burn it.

So far as I know, this example was first used in an article by Professor Alf Ross (*Ph. of Sci.*, 1944, p. 38). It seems at first sight

This paper was read to a colloquium on deontic logic at Manchester in 1965. I am grateful to the members of the colloquium, and also to Professor B. A. O. Williams, for helpful criticisms.

an extremely odd inference; and yet the indicative inference of the same form would be valid by the rules of ordinary logic: from 'You are going to post the letter' we can infer 'Either you are going to post the letter or you are going to burn it'. This latter inference has, indeed, been rejected by some critics of the ordinary propositional calculus; but it is now generally accepted as valid. From examples like this, some writers have argued that imperative logic must be radically different from ordinary logic. Some of them, confusing imperative logic with the logic of normative judgements, have gone on to argue the same for these latter (thereby reaching a correct conclusion, as I think it, by a mistaken argument).[1] Others have argued from the same examples that there cannot be imperative inferences.[2]

Professor Williams gives the key to the understanding of this problem when he says that in such imperative 'inferences' (which he rejects) the premiss has 'permissive presuppositions' (as he calls them) which are in some sense inconsistent with the 'permissive presuppositions' of the conclusion. If a person says 'Post the letter', we naturally take him to imply that we are not permitted not to post the letter. On the other hand, if a person says 'Post the letter or burn it', we naturally take him to imply that he permits us not to post the letter, so long as we burn it. The latter permission is inconsistent with what we have seen to be a 'permissive presupposition' of the premiss (the command to post the letter). Therefore, according to Williams, the premiss is actually inconsistent with the conclusion. He argues that therefore 'the successive utterance of the commands ... has a cancelling effect, the effect of withdrawing what has already been said; and that this feature is incompatible with construing such a sequence as an inference' (p. 33).

We may leave on one side the question of whether 'I permit you: not to do x, if you do y' *is* inconsistent, and in what sense, with 'I do not permit you not to do x'. Some might hold that they can be construed, jointly and consistently, as an oblique refusal of permission to do y or even as an oblique way of stating that the person addressed is not going to do y. But I shall not pursue this point.

In using the expression 'permissive presuppositions', Williams seems to incline to the view that these are not ordinary entail-

---

[1] See my review of E. W. Hall, *What is Value?*, in *Mind* (1954).
[2] E.g. B. A. O. Williams, *Anal. Supp.* (1963), p. 32.

ments. We must therefore ask whether the command 'Post the letter' *entails*, or only implies in some weaker sense, the withholding of permission not to post the letter, and similarly for the command to post the letter or burn it and the permission not to post it so long as we burn it. If these are not entailments, what are they?

We need not spend long on the logical relation between the command to post the letter and the withholding of permission not to post it. Although there might be further argument about this, I propose to take it that 'Post the letter' *entails* 'You may not refrain from posting the letter'. Another way of putting this is to say that 'Post the letter' is logically inconsistent with 'You may refrain from posting the letter'. This is an instance of what seems to be a general rule, that two commands, or a command and a permission, are logically inconsistent if the statement that one is going to be acted on is inconsistent with the statement that the other is going to be acted on – in other words, if it is logically impossible to act on both.[1]

I shall, however, argue that the relation between the command to post the letter or burn it and the permission not to post it so long as one burns it is not one of entailment; it is similar rather to those discussed by Grice.[2] There is (if I may summarise Grice's view rather crudely) a set of general conventions which have to be observed if communication is to work and misunderstandings, disharmonies and other failures of communication are to be avoided. These conventions are quite general; they do not depend on the particular meanings or logical properties of particular sentences or other utterances. Two of the most important of these conventions are, not to say things which are quite irrelevant to the point of the communication in the context, and not to omit things which are importantly relevant. It is the latter convention which especially concerns us.

The existence of these conventions means that, if we say some things, in some contexts, we imply (or, to adopt Grice's term, 'conversationally implicate') certain other things which we have left unsaid. Thus if (Grice's example) in reporting on a pupil, I say 'He has beautiful handwriting and his English is grammatical', and say no more, it will be taken that he is no good at philosophy. This is because the fact, if it were a fact, that he

[1] Cf. Williams, p. 30.   [2] *Ar. Soc. Supp.* (1961) pp. 126 ff.

was good at philosophy would be, in the context, highly relevant; therefore, by praising his writing and his English, but omitting to praise his philosophy, I am doing something which would be contrary to the general conventions of communication if in fact I were of the opinion that his philosophy was good too. I would be omitting an importantly relevant item from my communication although in a position to insert it. Because it is the general convention to refrain from doing this, it is assumed on the present occasion that the reason why I have not inserted any praise of my pupil's philosophy is that I am not in a position to do so; and that is why, by saying what I have said, I have 'implicated conversationally' that there is nothing to be said for his philosophy.

Similarly, if someone is asked where Jones is, and answers 'Somewhere in Scotland', when he knows that Jones is at 115 Dalkeith Road, Edinburgh, and that this is highly relevant, he is in breach of conversational good form. It is this convention which makes *suppressio veri* into *suggestio falsi*; witnesses undertake to observe it when they swear to speak 'the whole truth' – they are not swearing to utter the totality of true propositions, but rather, not to omit importantly relevant truths from their answers to questions.

The general principle is summarised by Grice, and applied to disjunctive utterances, as follows:

> One should not make a weaker statement rather than a stronger one unless there is a good reason for so doing ... On the assumption that such a principle as this is of general application, one can draw the conclusion that the utterance of a disjunctive sentence would imply the speaker's ignorance of the truth-values of the disjuncts, given that (*a*) the obvious reason for not making a statement which there is some call on one to make is that one is not in a position to make it, and given (*b*) the logical fact that each disjunct entails the disjunctive but not *vice versa*: which being so, the disjuncts are stronger than the disjunctive. (*Ar. Soc. Supp.*, 1961, p. 132)

What Grice says is applicable, *mutatis mutandis*, to imperative utterances; but let us start with an indicative example. If, being absent-minded, I ask my wife 'What have I done with the letter?' and she replies that I have posted it or burnt it, she conversationally implicates that she is not in a position to say which I have done; this is because, if she were in a position to make the stronger statement that I have posted it, she should have said so, it being obviously important which I have done. She also conversationally implicates that I may not have posted it, so long as I have burnt it.

If we put this example into the future tense, we come even closer to Williams's imperative case. From 'You are going to post the letter or burn it' we could, if we could think up a realistic context for such an utterance, get the conversational implicature 'You may be going not to post the letter, so long as you are going to burn it'. Now this latter might be thought in some sense inconsistent with the statement 'You are going to post the letter'. But we do not commonly hear it argued that the inference from 'p' to 'p or q' in the indicative mood is inadmissible because 'p' is inconsistent with a conversational implicature of 'p or q'. And there is no more reason to reject the corresponding imperative inference. If 'p or q' *entailed* propositions which were logically inconsistent with 'p', we should indeed have to reject the inference; but conversational implicatures do not have this effect. Therefore, it may be the case that, in the imperative mood also, there is a valid inference from 'Post the letter' to 'Post the letter or burn it', although the latter has a conversational implicature which is inconsistent with the former, and which amply explains, as in the indicative case, why such an inference would not in any normal context be used.

The matter can be further clarified in the following way.[1] If I want somebody to post the letter, it is up to me to say 'Post the letter'; if I gave the weaker command 'Post the letter or burn it', I should conversationally implicate that he may refrain from posting it, so long as he burns it. Therefore, if I tell him to post the letter, and he infers from this to 'Post the letter or burn it', and fulfils this latter command by burning the letter, he has erred. But his error consists, not in making an invalid inference, but in fulfilling the weaker command when what I gave him was the stronger. We cannot in general be sure of fulfilling commands by fulfilling other commands which are inferable from them. We cannot, for example, fulfil the command 'Put on your parachute and jump out' by just jumping out. In such cases, the inferred command gives a necessary, but not a sufficient, condition for fulfilling the command from which it is inferred. In this respect commands are just like statements,

[1] See further my review of E. W. Hall referred to above.

except that fulfilment takes the place of belief (which is the form of acceptance appropriate to statements). If I am told 'He has put on his parachute and jumped out', I am thereby licensed to accept or believe the statement which is inferable from it, 'He has jumped out'. But if I believe that that is all he has done, I am in error. Similarly, if I am told to put on my parachute and jump out, and think that all I have to do is to jump out, what is wrong with my inference is not the conclusion that I am to jump out; this is quite correct. What is wrong is the unjustified conclusion that this is all I have to do. I have supposed that the conclusion gives a sufficient condition of fulfilling the premiss, whereas it gives only a necessary condition. In the same way, in the indicative example, acceptance of the conclusion is a necessary condition for accepting the premiss, not a sufficient condition. One cannot, in consistency, accept the premiss without accepting the conclusion; but one can very well accept the conclusion without having accepted all that is in the premiss. Once this feature of all inferences, that the conclusion gives a necessary condition, not a sufficient one, is applied in the appropriate way to imperative inferences, the paradoxical character of inferences such as we have been considering vanishes.

In the case of the disjunctive inference with which we started, this is not so obvious, because it is not natural to say that the man who fulfils the command 'Post the letter or burn it' by burning it has fulfilled some part, but not the whole, of the command 'Post the letter'. It is more natural to say that he has fulfilled a command, the fulfilment of which is a necessary condition of fulfilling the command 'Post the letter', but not a sufficient condition. But the same principle applies. To sum up: the inference from 'Post the letter' to 'Post the letter or burn it' strikes us as paradoxical, (1) because the conversational implicatures of the second of these propositions are so much at variance with the first of them that the inference could have no normal use, and (2) because it is not realised that to fulfil the conclusion of an imperative inference is not necessarily to fulfil the premisses.

A similar move enables us to deal with another of Williams's examples (p. 31). In the propositional calculus, there is a valid inference from 'p or q' and 'not p' to 'q'. Many writers on the logic of imperatives, including myself, have admitted a similar inference with the premisses and conclusion in the imperative: i.e. an inference from 'Do *a* or do *b*' and 'Do not do *a*' to 'Do *b*'. Against this, Williams argues that the two premisses are in some sense inconsistent with one another. A 'change of mind' must have taken place between the two premisses, and so the inference is destroyed by this discontinuity. The reason why he says that the two premisses are, in the imperative case, inconsistent, is the following. The disjunctive imperative 'Do *a* or do *b*' has a permissive presupposition that the person addressed may do *a*; but the second premiss, 'Do not do *a*', has a permissive presupposition which is inconsistent with this, namely that he may not do *a*. Thus the two premisses, having mutually inconsistent permissive presuppositions, are themselves mutually inconsistent.

We may perhaps say, in the same way as before, that the relation between 'Do not do *a*' and 'You may not do *a*', which Williams says is one of permissive presupposition, is actually one of entailment; but I do not need to insist on this. On the other hand, as before, the relation between 'Do *a* or do *b*' and 'You may do *a*' is only a Gricean conversational implicature. The command 'Do *a* or do *b*' is weaker, in Grice's sense, than the command 'Do not do *a*; do *b*'; the latter entails the former, but not vice versa. Therefore, if the speaker wished the person addressed to do *b* but not *a*, it would be highly misleading of him to give the weaker command 'Do *a* or do *b*'. If, therefore, he does give this latter command, it is conversationally implicated that his wishes are not such as would be expressed by the command 'Do not do *a*; do *b*'. Therefore it is conversationally implicated that the person addressed may do *a*. And this implicature is inconsistent with the second premiss in the inference, namely 'Do not do *a*'. But, as before, it does not follow, from the fact that a proposition has conversational implicatures which are inconsistent with another proposition, that the two propositions cannot occur as constituents of the same valid inference.

In this case, the inference even has possible uses. They are made possible by a device to which Grice draws attention, and which he calls the *cancellation* of conversational implicatures.[1]

---

[1] Needless to say, this use of 'cancellation' is quite distinct from that in which some writers have said that the imperative 'Do *a*' can be 'cancelled' by saying 'You do not have to do *a*'.

That an implicature can be cancelled is treated by Grice as a sign that it is only a conversational implicature and nothing stronger. Suppose that I am a transport officer sending off a convoy from London to Edinburgh. There are five reasonably convenient routes: they all follow the Great North Road as far as Scotch Corner or thereabouts, and then they go respectively (read from west to east) via Beattock, Hawick, Carter Bar, Coldstream and Berwick. Only the last two (the two eastern ones) involve going through Newcastle. I do not know what the snow conditions on the border are, but I know that the Berwick route is certain to be all right, but is rather longer. I therefore say to the commander of the convoy 'Go via Coldstream or Berwick; I am not saying which at the moment, and I'm not authorising you yet to take the Coldstream route; report to the Transport Officer at Newcastle and he will give you a further message from me'. When he gets to Newcastle, I have found out that the Coldstream route is blocked, and so I send the message 'Don't go via Coldstream'. He therefore infers from the two premisses that I have given him, 'Go via Coldstream or Berwick' and 'Don't go via Coldstream', that he is to go via Berwick.

In this example, a conversational implicature, which the disjunctive imperative would normally have, is cancelled. Normally, if I said, *sans phrase*, 'Go via Coldstream or Berwick', I should be taken as authorising him to go via Coldstream if he thought fit. But what I actually said was 'Go via Coldstream or Berwick; I'm not saying which at the moment, and I'm not authorising you yet to take the Coldstream route; etc.' That I can say this without self-contradiction shows that 'Do a or do b' does not entail 'You may do a' but only conversationally implicates it. And from this it follows that, in the inference from 'Do a or do b' and 'Do not do a' to 'Do b', the two premisses are not inconsistent in the sort of way that Williams's argument requires. For exactly the same trick could be worked in the indicative mood; and nobody would wish to argue that therefore the corresponding inference in propositional logic is faulty. If I know, at one stage in my enquiry into a man's movements, that he is going to go via Coldstream or Berwick, and then discover at a later stage that he is not going to go via Coldstream, I can infer that he is going to go via Berwick. The disjunctive statement that he is going to go via Coldstream or Berwick does, indeed, carry in normal contexts the conversational implicature that he may be going to do either, and *this* is inconsistent, in some sense, with the later piece of information that he is not going to go via Coldstream; but the propositional calculus is unscathed.

If the parallelism between indicatives and imperatives is fully and correctly worked out, it will commonly be found that what is sauce for one is sauce for the other. Williams points to some differences between imperatives and indicatives; but it may be doubted whether these have the consequences which he alleges (p. 33). He argues first, that since it is up to a commander to decide what he wants, a movement from a less determinate to a more determinate command must signify a change of mind; if he had the more determinate want all along, it was up to him to say so to start with. He contrasts the case of indicatives, in which what is the truth does not depend upon the will of the speaker, and in which, therefore, new premisses giving new information can be added to the less determinate ones already available. But in the example given, the commander, *as a result of getting new information*, issues a new and more determinate command, which, however, is not inconsistent with the previous command as given, since the conversational implicatures of that were explicitly cancelled. He has not changed his mind.

Williams argues, secondly, that 'If a commander first gives a disjunctive command, and then moves to the negation of a disjunct, he is in effect calling the agent back, and starting again' (p. 34). But in the example given, the commander cannot be doing this, because what he has said already is a necessary ingredient in the total series of orders; without it, the recipient would not know what to do. The commander is therefore not cancelling his previous order; both the previous order and the subsequent one are required in order that from the combination of them the recipient may *infer* what he is to do.

Is such an inference, as Williams seems finally to suggest, not an imperative inference but a deontic one 'I must do a or b; I must not do a; so I must do b'? 'Must', we can agree, is different from imperatives, just as 'ought' is (see below). But suppose the recipient were to say 'I am to go via Coldstream or Berwick; I am not to go via Coldstream; so I am to go via Berwick'. Would these be deontic utterances? If (as we certainly should) we distinguish between imperative and deontic utterances, 'I am to' should clearly be put on the imperative side of the fence.

Perhaps what we need initially are more fences. But if the commander were rung up on the telephone by his subordinate and asked to make himself clear, might he not say, with some impatience, 'You are to go via Coldstream or Berwick; and you are not to go via Coldstream; so you are to go via Berwick' ? Would he not, then, be spelling out an imperative inference ? For it is hard to see much difference, in this context, between the two utterances 'You are to go via Berwick' and 'Go via Berwick'.

We must now consider the second group of temptations which have led people to say that the logic of imperatives is different from ordinary propositional logic. They all arise through a failure to distinguish between ordinary imperatives like 'Shut the door' and what may be called deontic or normative sentences like 'You ought to shut the door'. I shall be maintaining that the logic of these is quite different from one another. The logic of 'ought'-sentences seems to stand in somewhat the same relation to that of ordinary imperatives as does the logic of modal sentences to that of ordinary indicatives.[1] It is possible that the confusion between 'ought' and the imperative is due originally to the fact that the German word 'sollen' is used, in certain contexts, for both, and that some of the most influential early writers on the logic of imperatives were native speakers of German. There is no excuse for speakers of English, which distinguishes clearly between 'You ought to' and 'You are to', making this confusion.

People who make it are sometimes led to argue as follows. They find (perfectly correctly) that the logic of normatives differs from ordinary propositional logic. They then, because they have not distinguished imperatives from normatives, argue that therefore the logic of imperatives must be different from propositional logic. But the questions 'Is normative logic different ?' and 'Is imperative logic different ?' are not the same question; and the answer to the second may be 'No', even if the answer to the first is 'Yes'.

There are good reasons for holding that the logic of 'ought' is different from ordinary propositional logic. The first point of

[1] See H. N. Castañeda, *Ph. Studies* (1955); E. M. W. Fisher, *Mind* (1962); and my *Language of Morals*, p. 27 n. For the differences between imperatives and normatives, see my *Freedom and Reason*, p. 36, and *Language of Morals*, pp. 175 ff.

difference is that which has led people to say, either that the logic of 'ought' is three-valued, or that the law of the excluded middle does not apply to 'ought'-statements. It is possible for it to be neither the case that Smith ought to do a, nor the case that Smith ought not to do a; the proposition that Smith either ought to do a or ought not to do a is not a logical truth. It may be indifferent, as they say, whether Smith does a. But here there is a trap to be avoided. Let us for the moment forget about three-valued logics and operate with the connectives of ordinary logic, including ordinary negation. We shall then see that it is not necessary to speak of three-valued logic in this context (useful as it may be in others), and that it is not necessary here to invoke a special kind of negation. We need only to be clear-headed about the question, *What is* the negation or contradictory of an 'ought'-judgement?

The contradictory of 'Smith ought to do a' is not 'Smith ought not to do a', but 'It is not the case that Smith ought to do a'. And similarly the negation of 'Smith ought not to do a' is 'It is not the case that Smith ought not to do a'. We have, therefore, not three propositions, as in the above suggestions, but four. The two which begin 'It is not the case that . . .' are different, logically independent, propositions. The trap to be avoided is that of thinking that the proposition 'It is indifferent whether Smith does a' is a simple one; it is in fact equivalent to the conjunction of propositions 'It is not the case that Smith ought to do a, and it is not the case that Smith ought not to do a'.

Having got our four propositions, we can then arrange them on the lines of the old square of opposition, as is done by Professor Prior,[1] and we shall find that the relations between them are the same as in the old square (not that this is free from problems). 'Ought' and 'ought not' are contrary, not contradictory expressions; the contradictory of 'ought' is 'not the case that ought', and the contradictory of 'ought not' is 'not the case that ought not'. The fact that these deontic propositions fall into the same square as quantificational expressions is some support for the view that 'ought'-statements are universalisable; if the universalisability thesis is correct, it is what we should expect. It is significant that alethic modal propositions, which are also universalisable, fall into a similar square.[2] This, however, is not an appropriate place to embark on a discussion of

[1] *Formal Logic*, p. 220. [2] See Prior, op. cit., p. 187.

the relations between modal, quantificational and other propositions.

Let us now ask what is the place of permissions in this scheme. Corresponding to the above-mentioned confusion between 'ought' and imperatives, there is a similar confusion between two quite different things which have been called, in the books, permissions. The first is expressed in English by such phrases as 'It is all right to'. The second is expressed by 'You may', in that sense in which it means the same as 'I (hereby) permit you to'. 'You may', in this sense, expresses a permission given by a particular speaker, and is, as we might say, personal to him. The question of a reason for the permission need not arise, though it often does (compare the case of ordinary singular imperatives discussed in *Freedom and Reason*, loc. cit.). If the Shah of Persia says to a courtier 'You may go now', there has not got to be anything about the situation which makes it now appropriate to say this. On the other hand, if the Shah says 'It is all right for you to go now', the courtier is in order if he wonders what has changed in the situation to make it all right to go now, though it was not before. This shows that 'It is all right to' expresses more than a particular speaker's permission.

The expression 'It is all right to' fits quite easily into the square of opposition which we set up for 'ought'. We might say that 'It is all right for Smith to do a' means the same as 'It is not the case that Smith ought not to do a'.

Although it is quite wrong to say that 'It is all right to' expresses a permission (just as it is, for different reasons, wrong to say that all 'ought'-sentences, even in moral contexts, refer to obligations), we may bow to convention and use the symbols 'O' and 'P' to stand for 'It ought to be made the case that' and 'It is all right for it to be made the case that' respectively. But, if we do this, we must be constantly on our guard against thinking that 'Op' means 'Let it be the case that p' or that 'Pp' means 'It may be made the case that p'. Provided that one avoids this confusion, one can say that the square of opposition for deontic modalities can be written:

$$Op \qquad ONp$$
$$Pp \qquad PNp$$

One can perhaps treat 'P' as a defined operator meaning the same as 'NON'. There remains the question of what, in this symbolisation, the small '*p*'s and '*q*'s represent; but that I shall not discuss in this paper.

I have given reasons for thinking the logic of 'ought' and 'It is all right to' to be different from ordinary propositional logic and much more like a modal logic. We must now ask whether any of this is true of plain imperatives or 'may'. I shall argue that, in spite of appearances to the contrary, it is not true. Prima facie, it looks attractive to set up a similar square of opposition for ordinary imperatives, as follows:

Do *a*   Do not do *a*

You may do *a*   You may abstain from doing *a*

Here the 'may' is some sort of negation or (better) withholding of an imperative (affirmative or negative). We shall ask in a moment, what sort; and it will turn out to be a difficult question. Hall argued on these lines.[1] He wished to prove that imperative logic is different from indicative logic; and he tried to do this by pointing out that there is, as we might say, a *tertium* between 'Do *a*' and 'Do not do *a*'. For I do not have to tell a man to do *a* or tell him not to do *a*; I can let him do what he wants. Thus far all can agree; the question is, How is this to be interpreted?

Let us try to shed some light on the question by asking whether, after all, exactly the same trick cannot be played in the indicative mood. If this were so, the argument that imperative logic is different would break down. And in fact it can be played quite easily, using another sense of 'may'. Our square of opposition is then as follows:

The cat is on the mat   The cat is not on the mat

The cat may be on the mat   The cat may be not on the mat

But the questions remain, What is this 'may'? and What are the relations between the corners of the square?

It is easy to see that the 'square' which we have just set out bears only a slight resemblance to the ordinary square of opposition. 'The cat may be not on the mat' is not the contradictory of 'The cat is on the mat'; and 'The cat may be on the mat' is not the contradictory of 'The cat is not on the mat' – as would be the case if this square were like the ordinary one. If we are looking for the contradictory of 'The cat is on the mat', we find it in the wrong place; for the top two corners of the

[1] Op. cit.; see my review referred to above.

square, 'The cat is on the mat' and 'The cat is not on the mat', are not contraries, as they should be, but contradictories.

What is the relation between 'The cat is on the mat' and 'The cat may be not on the mat'? Certainly no relation known to ordinary propositional logic. The word 'may' has many different uses; but in one of them 'The cat may be not on the mat' might be rephrased 'I don't say that the cat is on the mat'. Is it possible that the function of 'may' in this sense is to *refuse* to say something? Suppose we are peremptorily asked 'State whether the cat is on the mat'; it may be impossible for us to do this, because we just do not know whether the cat is on the mat. Or we might have some other reason for not saying; if, during a game of hunt-the-thimble, I am asked by one of the children playing whether the thimble is near the window, I may properly answer 'It may be', even though I know very well where the thimble is. We have a use for a way of volubly and loquaciously *not* making a certain statement; and perhaps there is one sense of 'may' in which it fulfils this function.

We may doubt, therefore, whether the imperative square of opposition set out earlier really is the same sort of thing at all as the modal squares with which we started. For in many ways it is more like the indicative pseudo-square which we have just been discussing than it is like the modal squares. 'You may abstain from doing *a*' seems very like 'I don't tell you to do *a*'; and 'You may do *a*' seems very like 'I don't tell you not to do *a*'. And if we ask, which is the true contradictory of 'Do *a*': 'Don't do *a*' or 'I don't tell you to do *a*', I myself have no hesitation in answering 'The former'. I must now try to justify this lack of hesitation.

Consider the following objection. Surely, it might be said, I don't have to say either 'Do *a*' or 'Don't do *a*'. I can say 'It's up to you' or 'Do what you like' or a number of other things. Or, still more plausibly, the objector may say: If you consider the other way of giving commands, in the form 'You are to do *a*' and 'You are not to do *a*', surely it could *be the case* neither that the man spoken to is to do *a*, nor that he is not to do *a*. There is no injunction to him to do *a*, nor is there any injunction not to do *a*.

Now this way of putting the objection gets us to the heart of the difficulty. Indicative ways of speaking are very familiar to logicians, and they are always loth to abandon them. Those

IMPERATIVES AND INDICATIVES 39

who are, as we might put it, 'indicative-bound' will always have a hankering to ask 'Is it the case that p', even when 'p' stands for an imperative. If one insists on asking this question, one may get answers which miss the point – the essential nature – of imperatives. It cannot, literally, be the case that p, where 'p' stands for an imperative. I can *say* 'p', or I can *say* 'not-p'; and the logic of imperatives is about consistencies and inconsistencies between imperatives of this general sort, and about what we must in consistency agree to, if we have said something else.

Now if we translate 'Do a' as 'You are to do a' (as is in itself quite legitimate); and if we regard this as something that *is the case*, then we shall get puzzles about *what* exactly is supposed to be the case – puzzles that we should avoid if we can. It is, indeed, common form to use the phrase 'It is not the case that' as a way of negating an utterance; we used it above with 'ought'-statements, in order to express their negations, which, as we saw, cannot be expressed by saying 'ought not'. It is possible to do this, while remaining uncommitted about the logical status of the utterance which is negated. But when people say that it might be the case of somebody, neither that he is to do a, nor that he is not to do a, they are implicitly giving these imperatives the status of indicatives – of sentences which can express what is the case in a much stronger sense. In this they are supported, prima facie, by the fact that there is a sense of 'You are to' in which it means the same as 'Some person or authority, identifiable but not identified, has as a matter of fact commanded, or does as a matter of fact command, you to'. This is, in one of the senses of that ambiguous term, a metalinguistic statement; it reports the second-order fact that somebody has said or says something. And this is something that could *be the case* in the strongest possible sense.

If 'You are to' is taken in this way, then a ready sense can be given to 'It is the case that you are to'. But, fairly obviously, in this sense, 'You are to do a' does not mean the same as the ordinary imperative 'Do a'. For the latter is not (as on this interpretation the former is) a metalinguistic remark or report of what has been said. When I say 'Do a', I am not stating that the person addressed is or has been in fact commanded to do a; I am commanding him to do a.

Having removed this source of confusion, we can readily

admit that some of the things which our objector says about 'You are to do *a*' are true, in that sense of that expression in which it is *not* equivalent to the imperative 'Do *a*'. If no command has been issued, it is neither the case that the person in question has been commanded to do *a*, nor that he has been commanded not to do *a*. So 'You are to do *a*' and 'You are not to do *a*' are not contradictories, if they are taken as equivalent to 'You are as a matter of fact commanded to do *a*' and 'You are as a matter of fact commanded not to do *a*'. Obviously, the contradictory of 'You are as a matter of fact commanded' is 'You are as a matter of fact not commanded' and not 'You are as a matter of fact commanded not'.

However, all this is quite irrelevant to the question of whether 'Do *a*' and 'Do not do *a*' are contradictories; for, as we have seen, they are not the equivalents of the factual assertions just discussed. Reluctant as some extreme empiricists may be to admit it, 'Do *a*' can be a meaningful utterance without being a report of any fact. Confusion between the two uses of 'You are to' does, however, readily explain why it has seemed so plausible to say that 'Do *a*' and 'Do not do *a*' are not contradictories. The confusion creeps in, as I have said, because people ask 'Could there not be something that *was the case*, in between its being the case that you are to do *a* and its being the case that you are not to do *a* ?' To which the answer is 'Yes', if 'You are to do *a*' is taken as a factual report that a command has been given; but if it is taken as the equivalent of 'Do *a*', no sense has been given to the question; for the sentence 'It is the case that do *a*' has no meaning.

Coming back, then, to the original pair, 'Do *a*' and 'Do not do *a*', let us ask, yet again, whether they are contradictories. They seem to have as much right to be called contradictories as the corresponding indicative pair 'You are going to do *a*' and 'You are not going to do *a*'. If somebody asked me 'Am I to do *a*?', I could, of course, refuse to give him an answer; I could say 'I'm not telling you to do it, and I'm not telling you not to do it; decide for yourself'. And then it would be the case, neither that I had told him to do *a*, nor that I had told him not to do *a*. But similarly, if asked 'Is the cat on the mat ?', I could answer 'I'm not saying; you say'. And then it would be the case, neither that I had told him that the cat was on the mat, nor that I had told him that it was not. But if an answer (a straight answer) is insisted on in either case, then it must be a 'yes or no' answer. 'Tell me', the man might say, 'is the cat on the mat – yes or no?'; or 'Tell me, am I to do *a* – yes or no?'; and to questions like these, there is no third answer, in either case, besides 'Yes' and 'No'. I can remain silent, but that is no answer.

'But', our objector may say, 'surely this misses the point. In the indicative case, there is nothing that can *be the case* between the cat's being on the mat and the cat's not being on the mat, and this is what is meant by the law of the excluded middle. But in the case of the imperatives there is this something that could be the case, in between. For' (and this is where the indicative-bound cloven hoof shows itself) 'surely, if imperatives have a sense at all, there must be something that you are asserting to *be the case* when you utter an imperative – the *existence* of a norm, as perhaps Professor von Wright would put it. And if so, surely there is something in between the existence of the norm, to do *a*, and the existence of the norm, not to do *a*. For surely neither of these norms might exist.' But we can now see what is wrong with this whole approach. For to say 'Do *a*' is not to assert the existence of a norm, or of anything else. The reason why there seems to be a gap between what is *asserted* by 'Do *a*' and what is *asserted* by 'Don't do *a*' is not that they both make assertions, between which there is a gap; it is that neither of them makes any assertion at all. And this is because, being imperatives, it is not their job to make assertions. Another way of putting this point is as follows. Just as there is nothing I can *assert* in between 'The cat is on the mat' and 'The cat is not on the mat', so there is nothing I can *command* in between 'Do *a*' and 'Don't do *a*'.

We may therefore urge deontic logicians to take another look at the question of whether there are differences between indicative and imperative logic, keeping carefully in their minds, all the time, first of all the distinction between entailments and conversational implicatures; secondly, that between imperatives and normatives; and thirdly, that between commands and reports that a command has as a matter of fact been given.

By way of postscript, something needs to be said about a distinction which is of great importance for the logic of imperatives. Somewhat similar distinctions have been drawn by Ross in the paper referred to above, and by Mr Kenny in *Analysis*, XXVI, 3 (1966) 65. We may distinguish between a 'logic of satisfaction or fulfilment' for imperatives, and logics of 'validity' or 'satisfactoriness'. Both these kinds of logic would be attempts to find a 'value' which will play the part in imperative logic which is played by truth in indicative logic (for example, in the construction of truth-tables). Many would-be imperative logicians have been led astray by the search for such a truth-substitute; but the distinction is nevertheless important. In indicative logic, the premisses of a valid inference cannot be true and the conclusion false. If we recognise that commands cannot be true or false, it looks as if we have to find some notion to take the place of truth in the case of imperative inferences. The 'logic of satisfaction' makes use of the idea that in a valid imperative inference the premisses cannot be fulfilled or satisfied without the conclusion being satisfied. The logics of 'validity' and 'satisfactoriness' use, instead, the idea that the premisses of a valid imperative inference cannot be 'valid' or 'satisfactory' without the conclusion being so too. It is obvious that these two ideas will lead to quite different logics.

The logic of satisfaction is bound to be isomorphous with ordinary indicative logic. Indeed, it has been said with some justice to be nothing but an application of ordinary indicative logic. It may be that the imperative inferences considered above are all inferences in the logic of satisfaction, and therefore only indicative inferences in disguise. This should not alarm us; if the imperative inferences which we wish to make, and which are important for practical thinking, turned out to have this basis, that would be both a great simplification of the subject and at the same time an adequate support for prescriptive logic as applied in moral and other fields. A logic of satisfaction would still be an imperative logic in the sense that it would tell us how to know, when given a command, what other commands must necessarily be fulfilled if we are to fulfil the first command. And this is what we are looking for in most imperative inferences.

On the other hand, it may be doubted whether logics of validity or satisfactoriness can be called logics of imperatives at all. They are, rather, logics of modal statements *about* commands, such as statements that a certain command is valid or satisfactory. Without going into all the difficulties and problems raised by this suggestion, I will venture the opinion that, since there is nothing to correspond to truth in the case of commands, those who look for a kind of *ersatz* truth to form the basis of a logic of imperatives are looking in the wrong place.

What is needed, rather, is a logic which tells us what other things we are, implicitly, commanding when we give a certain command, just as ordinary logic tells us what other things we are, implicitly, asserting when we make a certain assertion. We want to be able to say: 'If you command that p, you are commanding, implicitly, that (at least) q'. For example, we want to be able to say: 'If you command that the letter be posted, you are commanding, implicitly, that it be at least posted-or-burnt'; or 'If you command a man to put on his parachute and jump out, you are commanding him, implicitly, (at least) to jump out'. The burden of this article has been that some of the reasons sometimes given for holding that such a logic could not be isomorphous with indicative logic are bad ones.

3 Wanting: Some Pitfalls

The first part of this paper is an attempt to find a hole in Professor Max Black's argument in his article 'The Gap between "Is" and "Should"'.[1] Let me start with a concrete example. Uncle John, an elderly and rich bachelor, and his nephew and sole heir James, are fishing from a small boat in shark-infested waters out of sight of other vessels. As they are waiting for a bite, James says:

James: Do you know, there's nothing in the world I want more than to have half a million dollars, and spend it on enjoying myself.

Uncle John: I suppose that's true. You could never do without women, and women are expensive these days. Besides, if you say that that's what you want, who am I to doubt your word? You have certainly been trying very hard lately to make money at the races, but you haven't had any luck.

J.: Yes; repeated failures in that and other directions have convinced me that the one and only way of getting half a million dollars is to push you out of the boat.

U.J.: I'm afraid you're right about that. You never were much good at honest toil.

J.: So you agree that I do want half a million dollars, and that the only way of getting them is to push you out of the boat. What do you think I should do, then?

U.J.: Well, since you want, more than anything else, to have half a million dollars, and since the one and only way of getting them is to push me out of the boat, I can only conclude that you should push me out of the boat.

[1] Max Black, 'The Gap between "Is" and "Should"', *Philosophical Review*, LXXIII (1964) 165–181. If, in the course of arguing that Black's inference schema is *invalid*, I suggest that certain other schemata are, by contrast, *valid*, I do so without confidence, and only because their plausibility, and their deceptive similarity to Black's schema, may explain why he thought it valid. Professor Gauthier has half-convinced me that they are invalid also.

First published in 'Agent, Action and Reason', *Proceedings of Western Ontario Colloquium*, ed. R. Binkley (1968).

J.: I quite agree with both your premisses and your reasoning; therefore, since I never disregard soundly-based advice, especially from uncles . . .
   (*Pushes U.J. out of boat*)

Now it seems obvious that there is something logically wrong, and not merely morally disreputable, about this dialogue. But *what* is wrong with it is not easy to say. Let me first reject some suggestions which I think do not go to the root of the matter. First, I would agree, if anybody wanted me to for the sake of argument, that it would make no difference whether the word 'should' were used in the dialogue or the word 'ought'. Secondly, our unease has nothing to do with any *moral* feelings we have about pushing people out of boats; neither party to the dialogue says anything relevant about morals, and we may suppose that Uncle John's natural aversion from being fed to the sharks has other sources than moral disapproval of murder. Morals just do not come into the matter; we should still find the argument odd even if we and both parties were quite amoral.

Thirdly, the argument is not odd because James must be presumed to have other higher or preferred ends which conflict with his attaining his half-million dollars by this means. He said, you remember, 'There's nothing I want more'. And fourthly, Uncle John could not have escaped from the argument by withdrawing from the advising role; for he was asked a straight question, 'What do you think I should do then?' If the conclusion follows from the premisses, he must give it.

I think, therefore, that we shall have to investigate the matter a bit more deeply. It may help us if we consider and contrast the following two remarks, both of which might be made to a friend dining in a restaurant:

(1) If you want sugar in your soup, you should ask the waiter.
(2) If you want sugar in your soup, you should get tested for diabetes.

The difference between the two remarks can be brought out, first, by noticing the entirely different grounds that would be given to justify them. The first would be justified by pointing out that the waiter has the only access to sugar. The second would be justified by arguing that an inordinate desire for sugar is a symptom of diabetes, and that those with diabetes should have it treated. Alternatively, we might bring out the difference in the following way: the first suggests that asking the waiter would be a means to having sugar in one's soup; the second does not suggest that getting tested for diabetes is a means to having sugar in one's soup.

The difference between these two kinds of 'If you want'-statements was pointed out by me in *The Language of Morals*,[1] and also by Jonathan Harrison,[2] who made the additional point that the consequent of the 'diabetes' hypothetical can be detached by using *modus ponens*, but that that of the 'waiter' hypothetical cannot. Thus, it is permissible to argue 'If you want sugar in your soup, you should get tested for diabetes; but you do want sugar in your soup; therefore you should (absolutely) get tested for diabetes'. But it is not permissible to argue 'If you want sugar in your soup, you should ask the waiter; but you do want sugar in your soup; therefore you should (absolutely) ask the waiter'. As we shall see in more detail later, that is what is wrong, both with the James–Uncle John dialogue, and with Max Black's article on which it is modelled. I say 'you should (absolutely)' in order to contrast it with 'you should, if you want sugar in your soup'.

Let us consider the meaning of 'If you want' in the two cases. In the 'diabetes' case, a first approximation would be to say that it means the same as 'If you, as a matter of psychological fact, have a desire'. I am very much inclined to deny that it means anything like this in the 'waiter' case. But we cannot clarify this question until we know more about what it is to have a desire. Mr Kenny has suggested, adopting a device of Professor Geach's, that to have a desire is to say-in-one's-heart an imperative.[3] This is, of course, artificial, and I do not in any case have to take over the suggestion in its entirety. Neither Kenny nor Geach, I think, wishes to suggest that thinking is sub-vocal mouthing. Their suggestion, though artificial, is illuminating, and its artificiality is, perhaps, no greater than that which we have to endure in all cases in which we want to give linguistic expression to something that we do not say but only think.

Thus, I may be thinking that the clock has just struck five,

[1] R. M. Hare, *The Language of Morals* (Oxford, 1952) pp. 34 ff.
[2] *Ar. Soc. Supp.*, XXVIII (1954) 111–34.
[3] Anthony Kenny, *Action, Emotion and Will* (1963) chaps 10–11.

but may *say* nothing, either out loud, or even sub-vocally. It is useful, indeed essential, to be able to isolate the *proposition* which expresses what I am thinking, or would express it if it were uttered. It may be going too far to say that this kind of thought cannot be had at all by a creature which could not in principle express it in words; but at any rate, if we want to display the logical relations between this thought and other thoughts, we cannot do so without first putting them into words. Thus, if I not only think that the clock has just struck five, but think that for that reason it must be just after five, because the clock strikes five at five o'clock only, the logic of my reasoning cannot be displayed without putting the propositions (premisses and conclusion) into words.

It is this second point which is most relevant to the case of practical inferences. Unless we make some such move as Kenny's, we shall not be able to display the logical relations between desires and other thoughts or expressions. Many people who have written on this subject have thought that the way to get desires into the logical machinery was to put in premisses of the form 'X wants (or desires) that p'. But this is as unpromising a move as it would be to try to set up the propositional calculus, operating, not with propositions like 'p', 'q' and 'r', but with propositions like 'X believes that p', etc. On Kenny's view, 'X wants sugar in his soup' is to be rendered 'X says in his heart "Let me have sugar in my soup"'. We do not need, however, to employ quotation marks, which may seem objectionable, as suggesting sub-vocal speech. We can say 'X wants that he have' (note the mood) 'sugar in his soup'. Here the subordinate *oratio obliqua* clause 'that he have sugar in his soup' stands for what in *oratio recta* would be an imperative; if we were translating 'wants that he have sugar in his soup' into Urdu, the construction used would be that appropriate to an indirect command. And indeed, in Urdu, as in English, if we are reporting in indirect speech a command given by somebody else, we may say to the person commanded 'So and so *wants* you to do such and such'. So there is good reason for allowing that, whether or not the man who wants something 'says anything in his heart', an appropriate expression in language for what he is thinking, if we are to have one, is an imperative.

Now let us consider the 'diabetes' example with this point in mind. The inference seems to go like this (if you will tolerate for the moment Kenny's artificial translation): If anyone does as a matter of fact say-in-his-heart 'Let me have sugar in my soup', he should get tested for diabetes; but X (the man in question) does, as a matter of fact, say-in-his-heart 'Let me have sugar in my soup'; therefore X should get tested for diabetes. This is relatively unproblematical. It is the actual occurrence, in fact, of this thought in his heart which entitles us to detach the consequent of the hypothetical. But when we come to the 'waiter' example, the situation is different. There, what entitles us to detach the consequent is not the mere fact of X's saying-in-his-heart 'Let me have sugar in my soup'. Before we can *ourselves* affirm absolutely 'X should ask the waiter', *we* have to be, like X, saying-in-our-hearts 'Let X have sugar in his soup'. In fact, the real premiss in the argument is not the factual statement that X wants, or says-in-his-heart, what he wants or says; the real premiss is *what* he is saying in his heart – the thought that he is having, not the fact that he is having it. From this it follows that the consequent of a 'waiter'-type hypothetical 'should'-statement is detachable only by someone who is prepared himself to subscribe to the imperative which is implicitly contained in the conditional clause.

There is a subsidiary difficulty here which I am not going to try to deal with. Clearly there is a difference between the two utterances 'If you want sugar in your soup, *you should ask* the waiter', and 'If you want sugar in your soup, *ask* the waiter'. This difference has something to do with the universalisability of hypothetical 'ought'- and 'should'-statements; but I am not able to clarify it at the moment. However, I think that we are now in a position to explain both the plausibility of Max Black's argument and the strangeness of the Uncle John dialogue which is of the same form.

The plausibility of this form of argument (provided that the right instances are chosen for illustrating it) stems from the fact that it is easy to insert into it a step consisting of a proposition which seems to be both analytically true and sufficient to guarantee the validity of the argument. Black's example is:

Fischer wants to mate Botwinnik;
The one and only way to mate Botwinnik is for Fischer to move the Queen;
Therefore Fischer should move the Queen.

WANTING: SOME PITFALLS

Into this argument we might insert the apparently analytic step:

(a) If the one and only way to mate Botwinnik is for Fischer to move the Queen, then, if Fischer wants to mate Botwinnik, he should move the Queen.

This might be thought to be merely a particular case of the general analytic truth:

(a') If the one and only way to achieve a certain end is to adopt a certain means, then, if anybody wants to achieve the end, he should adopt the means.

This is, however, one of Satan's cleverest sophisms, and many there be who have gone to hell through being beguiled by it – like James in the dialogue. For the sense in which this is analytic is the sense which makes the second half of it ('if anybody wants to achieve the end, he should adopt the means') analogous to the 'waiter' hypothetical. In this sense, it is a complete justification of the proposition that if anybody wants E he should do M, to say that M is the only way of achieving E. But in *this* sense the consequent is not detachable. In order to make it detachable, we have to take 'if anybody wants to achieve the end, he should adopt the means' in a sense analogous to that of the 'diabetes' hypothetical. This is the sense we have to give the words, therefore, if we want to make the conclusion 'Therefore Fischer should move the Queen' a valid conclusion from the premisses

Fischer wants to mate Botwinnik

and

If Fischer wants to mate Botwinnik, he should move the Queen.

But in *this* sense neither (a) nor (a') is analytic. The Fischer-Botwinnik argument, therefore, has a premiss which is not only suppressed but equivocal; taken one way, it is analytic and hardly needs stating, but is insufficient to validate the argument; taken the other way, it validates the argument, but is not analytic.

The consequent of a 'waiter'-type hypothetical is detachable by putting in an *imperative* premiss. In the Uncle John case, this would be of the form 'Let James have half a million dollars'; in the Fischer–Botwinnik case it would be of the form 'Let Fischer mate Botwinnik'. It is because Uncle John obviously would not (in the circumstances) assent to this imperative premiss that the dialogue with which I started seemed so strange. It is because Uncle John does not want, more than anything else (even his own survival), that James should have half a million dollars, that he has not really got the logical wherewithal to enable him to detach the consequent which says that James should push him out of the boat. The *statement* that *James* wants this is not enough. For what would really make possible the detachment of the consequent is not *the fact that* James says-in-his-heart 'Let me have half a million dollars', but the thing that he says in his heart. Uncle John has to say this thing in his own heart before the *modus ponens* machinery will operate for him – for nobody can be compelled to assent to the conclusion of even a valid inference unless he accepts all its premisses.

But, it may be objected, is this true of the Fischer–Botwinnik inference? Has the speaker of this inference got himself to assent to the imperative which is being assented to or said-in-his-heart by Fischer when he wants to mate Botwinnik? I would answer, 'In a manner of speaking, yes'. Suppose that a spectator of the game very much wants Fischer not to move the Queen (perhaps he has a large bet on what Fischer's next move will be). He can follow this strategy:

(1) He assents to 'If Fischer wants to mate Botwinnik he should move the Queen' only in the 'waiter' sense (which is the only sense in which he can be compelled to accept it, given that the one and only way, etc.).

(2) He then refuses to accept the imperative premiss which, on this interpretation, is needed to detach the consequent 'Fischer should move the Queen'. This premiss is 'Let Fischer mate Botwinnik'.

No doubt this spectator could be compelled to assent to the conclusion 'Fischer should move the Queen' in the sense in which it is elliptical for 'If Fischer wants to mate Botwinnik, he should move the Queen' (taken in the 'waiter' sense). But in that case he would have assented only to a covertly hypothetical 'should', not to a categorical one. I do not think that many people would wish to deny that hypothetical 'should'-statements can be derived from 'is'-statements. It is the categorical 'should'-conclusion that is the real quarry; and that has escaped. And I may add in passing that, even if Black had caught his quarry in the Fischer–Botwinnik case, he would be very far from having proved the validity of the inference about pain which he inserts right at the end of his article. But that is another story.

I have, in the above, made some use of Kenny's idea that to have a desire is to say something (namely an imperative) 'in one's heart'. I am not committing myself to Kenny's account of wanting or of intention in its entirety. What I have said is that if we are going to talk about the logical relations between intentions or between wishes in the same sort of way as we sometimes do talk about the logical relations between beliefs, it is necessary to have a form of words which expresses the intention or the wish, or at any rate expresses it *if* it is expressed; and that the imperative sentence is a suitable form of words. I may remark in passing that, if we do express wishes in words, this enables us to distinguish between two sorts of wishes which do need distinguishing, namely those which are naturally expressed in the imperative, and those which are naturally expressed in various 'optative' constructions (e.g. 'Would that I were a bird!'). This supports Miss Anscombe's distinction[1] between the kind of wanting of which 'the primitive sign is trying to get', and 'idle wishing'. We might say that the latter is idle, unlike the former, because its expression, unlike an imperative, does not command any action.

Just as two beliefs are mutually inconsistent if their expressions in statements would be mutually inconsistent, so two desires are mutually inconsistent if their expressions in the imperative mood would be mutually inconsistent. I cannot rationally think that p and that not p, because 'p and not p' is self-contradictory; and I cannot rationally want (in the non-idle sense) that p and that not p, because the command that p and not p is self-contradictory. And just as we could not account for the mutual inconsistency of the beliefs that p and that not p by saying that 'x believes that p and x believes that not p' is self-contradictory (for it is not), so we cannot account

[1] G. E. M. Anscombe, *Intention*, 2nd ed. (Oxford, 1957) pp. 66 f.

for the mutual inconsistency of the desires that p and that not p by saying that 'x wants that p and x wants that not p' is self-contradictory; for that is not self-contradictory either.

There is, of course, a tiresome problem about the relations between the desire that p, which is not a speech-act, and the expressed command or request that p, which is. However, I do not feel called upon to say anything about this problem, because it is a quite general problem about the relations between thought and speech, affecting assertions and commands alike. This might be the subject of another paper, but I shall not attempt to deal with it in this one. I do not see that there is here any problem peculiar to imperative speech-acts. However, since I am advocating an account of the relation between desires and their expression in language which owes something to Kenny's, though it is not identical with his, it is perhaps apposite to say something in answer to various objections which have been made against Kenny's account, whether or not my own is exposed to them.

The first objection I wish to consider is made by Mr Pears.[1] He is criticising the view that *intentions* are the sayings-in-the-heart of commands. There are, of course, important differences between desires and intentions, and it is not to be assumed that what can be said of one can be said of the other. Nevertheless, Pears's criticism of this theory is worth examining. He puts the theory he is attacking in the following form: '"I intend to do A", when it is a genuine report of a state of mind, is tantamount to the statement " I have said in my heart, 'Let me do A'".' This is not a very fair statement of the theory, for it exposes it gratuitously to the objection that a man might have said in his heart 'Let me do A', and then, afterwards, changed his mind and said (also in his heart) 'No, let me not do A after all'. Such a man would have said in his heart 'Let me do A', but would not now intend to do A. However, let us ignore this complication, and suppose that the theory is not what Pears says it is, but rather, that the man who intends to do A is the man who in his heart *subscribes* (not necessarily sub-vocally and not necessarily occurrently) to the command 'Let me do A'.

Pears says of the theory 'The kind of command that is meant must be self-exhortation'. It is not clear to me why he says this,

[1] D. F. Pears, 'Predicting and Deciding', *Proceedings of the British Academy* (1964) pp. 203 f.

for he gives no reasons. Since the brunt of his subsequent argument against the theory depends on its being this particular kind of command that is in question, he surely owed it to Kenny to justify his choice of this implausible candidate. Exhortation is in fact a rather special use of the imperative mood. As Pears says, 'To exhort oneself to do something is a way of getting oneself to decide to do it'. This statement, which might be generalised to cover all exhortations and not just self-addressed ones, is another way of putting the point that an exhortation is, in Austin's term, at least partly a perlocutionary act. I say 'at least partly', because it might plausibly be maintained that an exhortation is also an illocutionary act; for the man who says 'I exhort you to do A' seems to be performing (at least as part of what he does) an illocutionary act of the same genus as that which includes requesting, ordering and praying – i.e. the genus of speech-acts that are typically done in the imperative mood.

It seems to me to be a mistake, however, to suppose that *all* speech-acts of this genus are also, essentially, perlocutionary acts, even in part. It is certainly extremely common to find philosophers saying that commands are, essentially, ways of *getting* people to do things. Professor Black even refers to them as verbal prods or pushes.[1] But the philosophers who say this sort of thing usually do so because they have not sufficiently studied Austin's distinction; and this cannot be true of Pears.

That a command is not essentially – though it may be commonly – a way of getting people to do things, was argued by me at some length in a paper a long time ago.[2] I think that I was there making in other words the same distinction as Austin called the illocutionary–perlocutionary distinction. On one of the very few occasions on which he read a paper in public about this distinction (at a colloquium organised by the British Council in Oxford in 1955), Austin was kind enough to say that he was saying the same sort of thing as I had been saying, and I think it was to this article he was referring. Neither as I made it, nor as he made it, is it free from difficulties, and there are annoying overlapping cases, of which exhorting is one and warning is another, which will continue to give trouble until we are a lot clearer about the basis of the distinction.

However, it ought to be clear at least that it is not true of

[1] Black, op. cit., pp. 172 f.
[2] R. M. Hare, 'The Freedom of the Will', *Ar. Soc. Supp.*, xxv (1951) 201.

commands in general that the person who issues them is, *ex vi termini*, trying to get people to do the things specified. The sadistic schoolmaster, who commands his boys to keep silent in the hope that this will cause them to talk so that he can beat them, is still commanding or telling them to keep quiet. Even if, as Miss Anscombe thinks and as I agree, 'the primitive sign of wanting is trying to get', and even if, as Kenny argued, wanting is to be represented as saying-in-the-heart an imperative, it does not follow that imperatives themselves are to be defined as verbal attempts to get. The man who wants that p says in his heart (on this view) 'Let it be the case that p'; and if this is what he is really saying in his heart, he *will* try to bring it about that p. But the saying of the imperative is not itself, essentially, an attempt to bring it about that p. How could it be, if the saying is only in the heart, and p is some external event like being given a drink?

Coming back, however, to the case of intending, with which we are at present concerned, it seems clear that if Kenny were to choose, not exhortation, but some other kind of command, as the kind that is being said in the heart when a man forms an intention, he would escape Pears's objection. This is stated as follows:

> To exhort oneself to do something is a way of getting oneself to decide to do it, or else a way of keeping oneself up to the mark after one has decided to do it: to form an intention is neither of these things.[1]

This seems to me true; it is at any rate not far from the truth to say that forming an intention and deciding are the same thing; and therefore, if exhorting oneself is a different thing from deciding, it must be a different thing from forming an intention. But the argument touches Kenny no more than it would touch somebody who maintained the surely irrefutable thesis that when Hannibal orders his troops to march on Rome he is commanding them to march on Rome. Here, too, if we made the gratuitous assumption that the kind of command that is meant 'must be' exhortation, we could argue that ordering cannot be this kind of commanding, and therefore (on this assumption) cannot be any kind of commanding, because to exhort is different from ordering.

[1] Pears, op. cit., p. 207.

That exhorting and ordering are different could easily be shown. Hannibal might first order his troops to march, and then, in an effort to get them to carry out his orders, exhort them to march. Or, if they were well disciplined and did not need exhorting, he might just order and not exhort them. If, on the other hand, they were so mutinous that an order from him would be the very thing that would stop them marching, he might refrain from ordering them but just exhort them – perhaps enlarging on the beauties of the Roman women. If we found such a scandalous inducement reported in Livy prefaced by the words '*hortatus est*', we should not be surprised. But the distinctness of ordering from exhorting does nothing to establish the distinctness of ordering from commanding, unless the assumption is made that 'the kind of command that is meant must be exhortation'.

The point is that commanding and ordering are illocutionary acts, but exhorting is essentially at least partly a perlocutionary act – an act of trying to get. Therefore the illocutionary act of ordering or in general of commanding is separable from the perlocutionary act of exhorting. So to prove that intending is not self-exhortation is not to prove that it is not self-commanding.

Actually it is very plausible to say that when Hannibal orders his troops to march on Rome he is not merely commanding them to do so, but expressing the intention that they should do so; and this lends some plausibility to the thesis that when I form the intention to go to Rome, I have that in my mind which would, if expressed in words, naturally be expressed by saying 'Let me go to Rome', or, if I were to address myself in military style in the mood which I was taught in the Army to call the future imperative, 'Hare will go to Rome', or 'I will go to Rome'.

Though it is easy to see why Pears thought his argument cogent, given that he thought that the self-addressed command in question was a perlocutionary act, it is not so easy to account for his adopting the following subsidiary argument. He says:

> Conveying information is not the primary purpose of self-exhortation, whereas it is the primary purpose of the two utterances ['I will do *A*' and 'I intend to do *A*'].[1]

It seems to me that this lacks at any rate the appearance of cogency as an argument against Kenny's view; for on Kenny's

---

[1] Ibid., pp. 207 f.

view 'I intend to do *A*' *would* have the primary purpose of informing (viz. of the fact that I subscribe to the self-addressed command to do *A*); and, on the other hand, 'I will do *A*', which is on Kenny's view not primarily informative, is *indeed* not primarily informative, but rather an expression of an intention or resolve. So Kenny, at least as far as concerns the primary informative purpose, or lack of it, of these two utterances, gets it right both times. Pears, on the other hand, seems to think that they are both primarily informative – which is false; and he seems to think – which is also false – that Kenny is required by his view to say that they are both primarily non-informative.

I have already touched on the fact that there are different sorts of commands, in the generic sense of that term; and I must now say more about this in order to counter one of several objections made by Mr D. R. Bell[1] against Kenny's views and my own. In the ordinary sense, commands, like orders (which are not the same thing), are distinguished from requests and prayers and other species of the genus to which they all belong, namely, the genus of speech-acts typically expressed in the imperative mood. This, I say, is the ordinary sense of the word 'command'. If I *ask* you to shut the door, I am not, in this ordinary sense, giving you a command. Now we do not have, in ordinary untechnical English, a single word for the genus I have just mentioned (though we have a generic *verb* for these speech-acts, namely 'tell to'). I now like to use the word 'imperation' for the genus of 'tellings to', meaning, roughly, 'speech-act for which an imperative is a natural form'. But in the traditional grammar-books we find the word 'command' used generically in this sense. For example, if I had to translate into Latin either the sentence 'He ordered his troops to pursue the enemy', or the sentence 'He begged her to stay', or the sentence 'He prayed to God to save him', I should in all these cases use one of the constructions which you will find classified in Kennedy's Latin Primer as 'indirect commands'. Having been brought up on this excellent book, I thought that it would be sufficient, when using the word 'command' for the genus in my book *The Language of Morals*, simply to spend one paragraph at the beginning of the book making this clear.

I did not, however, succeed in making it clear to Mr Bell; for although he quotes from this very paragraph, he does not

[1] D. R. Bell, 'Imperatives and the Will', *Ar. Soc.*, LXVI (1965–6) 129.

quote the sentence in which I say that I am going to use the word 'command' generically like the grammarians, but proceeds to take 'command' in the sense of 'order' in expounding and attacking my views. He does the same to Kenny, who has also done his best to make himself clear. Bell therefore spoils a promising article by attacking a non-existent target who thinks that intentions are self-addressed orders. Since he also makes the mistake mentioned above of interpreting orders as attempts to get something done (a view which he curiously attributes to Austin), he is evidently in some confusion about Austin's illocutionary–perlocutionary distinction. He even at one point, within three lines, says that orders are *il*locutionary acts and have the function of getting something done.[1]

Those of Bell's objections to Kenny and myself which are not vitiated by the above confusions take the form of alleged vicious regresses. There are two of these, so similar that it is hard to tell them apart. One of them goes: if the performance of a voluntary act involves addressing an order to oneself, then this in turn, being also a voluntary act, involves addressing to oneself an order to address the order, and so on. The other goes: if intending an act is addressing to oneself an order, then if obeying the order is also a voluntary act, there must also be an order, addressed to oneself, to obey the order, and so on. That these regresses (if they are really more than one) are spurious is indicated by the fact that they can be generated without bringing in the 'Imperative Theory of the Will' or referring to 'orders' at all, simply by using the words 'intend' or 'form an intention' themselves. Thus: (1) if the performance of a voluntary act involves forming an intention, then this in turn, being also a voluntary act, involves forming an intention to form the intention, and so on; (2) if intending an act involves forming an intention, then, if carrying out the intention is also a voluntary act, the agent has to form a second intention to carry out the first intention, and so on. It is not incumbent upon me to solve either of these regresses, since they arise independently of my views; they do not look too difficult to solve, but I shall be interested to hear people's views on them.

I will sum up this somewhat loosely knit paper by merely listing the pitfalls which I have been trying to mark. There is first of all the mistake of supposing that we can establish the

[1] Ibid., pp. 140 f.

statement 'I want to do *A*' as if it were a *statement about* a desire, but then use it as a premiss of inferences as if it were an *expression of* a desire (a role more naturally performed by an imperative); secondly, there is the confusion between commands as a genus and commands as a species of that genus; thirdly, there is the assumption that commands are essentially perlocutionary acts; fourthly, there is the refusal to allow liberties, in speaking of mental imperative 'speech-acts', that most of us allow in speaking of mental indicative 'speech-acts'. This last pitfall I merely marked, and did not discuss.

4 Practical Inferences

It is paradoxical that Alf Ross should be well known, both as a penetrating critic of the notion of 'Practical Reasoning', and as one who has made outstanding contributions to the study of the logic of imperatives. I therefore thought it fitting to write for this volume in his honour a discussion of one central question concerning that logic – a question, recent treatments of which have, inevitably, drawn on his seminal earlier work on the subject.

Whenever we are told to do anything, or whenever we ourselves form the intention of doing something, the question arises of how to do this, unless (as in the case of very simple commands or intentions) the answer is so obvious that the question does not need to be asked. There are, however, a number of distinctions which need to be made between different sorts of questions, all of which could be expressed in the phrase 'How shall I do this?' First, there is the distinction between *logical* conditions for being said to have done the thing in question, and *causal* conditions which have to be fulfilled if we are to do it. For example, if I am told to bring four sticks, it is a logical condition of doing this that I should bring at least three sticks; and if I am told to bring some water, it is a causal condition of this that I should get hold of a receptacle – but only a causal, not a logical condition, because a magician might be able to conjure water from place to place without receptacles.

Secondly, there is the distinction between logically or causally *necessary* conditions for performing the action, and logically or causally *sufficient* conditions for performing it. Thus, both the conditions mentioned in the preceding paragraph are necessary conditions; and on the other hand if I am told to bring *some* sticks, then bringing *these particular* sticks is a logically sufficient condition for doing as I am told; and if I am told to boil the water, putting the water in a receptacle on top of a fire that is of above a certain intensity is a causally sufficient condition for doing so.

First published in *Festskrift til Alf Ross*, ed. V. Kruse (1969).

In the case of most commands and intentions, we could not set about fulfilling them at all unless we could reason from them to the necessary and sufficient conditions for fulfilling them. This is because most commands are to at least some extent logically complex, and because nearly everything that we achieve is achieved indirectly, by initiating a causal process. It is the first reason that will mainly concern us in this paper. If I am told never to leave the door open, I cannot know what I have to do or to refrain from doing in order to obey this prohibition, unless on particular occasions I am able to reason: 'I am *never* to leave the door open; therefore I am not to leave it open *now*.' This conclusion gives a logically necessary condition of fulfilling the universal prohibition expressed in the premiss. Some of the inferences required will be less elementary than this; for example, if I am told to buy just enough glass wool to insulate a roof 24 ft wide and 60 ft long, and that it is only to be had in rolls 4 ft wide and 60 ft long, I have to be able, in order to fulfil this command, to reason that a logically necessary and sufficient condition of obeying the command, given this condition, would be to buy six rolls.

I propose to examine in this paper the light that is shed on the logic of imperatives by carefully observing the distinction between necessary and sufficient conditions. I shall not, therefore, say anything about a great many other distinctions which philosophers have thought important – and which are important – in this field, such as that between fiats and directives (Hofstadter and McKinsey, *Phil. of Science*, 1939); sentences and statements or commands (Bar-Hillel, *Analysis*, XXVI 3, 1966–7, among others); commands as speech-acts of commanding and commands as what is commanded (N. Rescher, *The Logic of Commands*, p. 8); satisfaction of commands and obedience to commands; commands in the generic sense in which they include, e.g., requests, and commands in the specific sense in which they do not. I mention these distinctions only in order that I may not be accused of being unaware of them and of others which, important as they are for many purposes, I do not think it relevant to mention here.

Aristotle, in the few places in which he discusses practical inferences, gives inadequate attention to the distinction between necessary and sufficient conditions. Consider, for example, the famous passage on practical syllogisms in *Movement of Animals* 701 a7ff. There we have the following inference:

> All men are to march
> I am a man
> ___
> (He at once marches)

where the conclusion is the action upon (or at least in accordance with) the imperative 'I am to march', which is, we might say, the logical conclusion of the inference. Here it is clear that, given that I am a man, my marching is a necessary condition for fulfilling the requirement that all men are to march. It is not a sufficient condition, because *my* marching will not fulfil that requirement unless everybody else does.

On the other hand, a few lines further down, we have the inference:

> A good thing is to be made by me
> A house is a good thing
> ___
> (He at once makes a house).

It is obvious that here the man in question is not fulfilling a necessary condition, but only a sufficient one, of making a good thing. There are a great many other alternative things which, if he made them, would fulfil the first premiss.

In another inference given in the same passage the two modes of inference are mixed:

> (1) I must have a covering
> A cloak is a covering
> ___
> I must have a cloak
>
> (2) I am to make what I must have
> I must have a cloak
> ___
> I am to make a cloak –

a conclusion which, Aristotle says, *is* an action. Here in (1) the reasoning is to a sufficient condition (for there are other coverings beside cloaks); but in (2) it is to a necessary condition (for if, as the Greek seems to imply, 'what' in the first premiss means 'everything that', the man will not have fulfilled it just by making *one* thing that he must have; however, in order to fulfil it, it is necessary that he should make this thing).

It would be tedious to examine Aristotle's other examples,

which will be found to be some of the 'necessary' type and some of the 'sufficient'. Without accusing him of being unaware of the distinction, we can at least complain of his lack of attention to it in this context; and the fault has infected subsequent writers. Once we are clear about the distinction, we can become a great deal clearer about the question, much discussed in recent years, of whether there can be practical inferences at all, and if so, whether the logic which governs them is the same as that which governs ordinary inferences from one statement to another statement, or whether it is radically different.

One approach to this question which has rightly attracted a great deal of notice is that of Mr Kenny, my debt to whom will already have become obvious (*Analysis*, XXVI 3, 1965-6). Taking over, and modifying, a very important distinction made by Alf Ross many years ago (*Phil. of Science*, XI, 1944), he points out that there is one kind of 'imperative inference' which could not be any different in its rules from ordinary assertoric or indicative inferences – namely that kind which is made according to what Ross and he call 'the logic of satisfaction'. Since to any imperative there corresponds an indicative to the effect that the imperative is 'satisfied' (which means that the thing which in the imperative is commanded to be made the case is the case), it must always be possible to reason in accordance with ordinary assertoric logic from a premiss to the effect that a certain imperative is satisfied to the conclusion that a certain other imperative is satisfied. For example, from the premiss that the command 'Do *a* and do *b*' is satisfied, we can infer the conclusion that the command 'Do *a*' is satisfied, since this inference merely puts in another form the inference from '*a* is done and *b* is done' to '*a* is done'. Note that even this modest form of 'imperative logic' (if that is what it is; Ross would perhaps deny it the name) requires imperatives to have *some* logical properties – namely those which entitle us to get from the formulation ' "Do *a* and do *b*" is satisfied' to the formulation '*a* is done and *b* is done', and from '*a* is done' back to ' "Do *a*" is satisfied'. But to this point I shall return.

Strictly speaking, the indicative which corresponds to an imperative (i.e. that which differs from it only in mood) is in the future tense, since imperatives themselves are future (the commands which they express are intended to be obeyed *after* their utterance). It might therefore be better if, instead of 'is satisfied', we wrote 'is going to be satisfied'. But for convenience of exposition I shall stick to the practice of Ross and Kenny.

Another way of describing the 'logic of satisfaction' (which puts essentially the same point in different terminology) is to say that in this logic 'satisfaction' is a value which is preserved in the same way as truth is in ordinary assertoric inferences. Just as, in valid assertoric inferences, if the premisses are true the conclusion is true, so, in an imperative inference in the logic of satisfaction, if the imperative premisses are satisfied and the indicative premisses (if any) true, then the imperative conclusion is satisfied.

The 'logic of satisfaction' is bound to be isomorphic with standard assertoric logic, as both Ross and Kenny make clear; and such a logic has been worked out in detail by Hofstadter and McKinsey (op. cit.). But though Kenny follows Ross almost exactly in his account of this 'logic of satisfaction', he makes a different choice of a logic to contrast it with. Ross contrasts it with a 'logic of validity' – a logic, that is to say, which proceeds from premisses of the form 'i_1 is valid' to conclusions of the form 'i_2 is valid', where i_1 and i_2 are two commands. Ross rightly distinguishes further between a perfectly comprehensible sense of 'valid' in which it means 'actually demanded or accepted by some specified or specifiable person' and another much more dubious sense in which it might mean 'objectively valid'. The latter sense he rejects on the ground that there is no empirical test for objective validity.

If 'i_1 is valid' means no more and no less than 'A (the person specified) accepts or demands i_1', it is an assertion and not an imperative; and, as such, it is obviously subject to ordinary assertoric logic. But (as Ross points out) there is not much that can be done with the logic of validity, as so interpreted. For it is by no means obvious how we can get from 'A demands i_1' to any other assertion of the form 'A demands i_2' (where i_1 and i_2 are different commands) without making certain quite contingent assumptions about the person A. We can, of course, get some conclusions out of the premiss 'A demands i_1' – for example, the conclusion that it is not the case that A does not demand i_1, or the conclusion that either A demands i_1 or p (where 'p' can be any other proposition). But (as the point might be put) because the command i_1 occurs in an intentional context, it is insulated from any logical operations and has to be transferred *en bloc* to any conclusions that may be drawn. But what we want is to get from the statement that A demands i_1 to the statement that A demands i_2, where i_1 is some command *different* from i_1 (if only in the way in which 'not-not-p' is different from 'p'). Yet so far we have not been shown even how, given that A demands i_1, we can infer that A demands not-not-i_1, nor that he does not demand not-i_1. People have been known to demand what they logically cannot have. To this point too we shall return.

It is Ross's contention that the appearance that the 'logic of validity' can do more than it really can is created by illegitimately *combining* elements of this logic with elements from the logic of satisfaction. Since his own article puts this point as clearly as it could be put, I shall not repeat his arguments here. I shall ask later whether there might, after all, be a legitimate way of combining elements from the two logics. But first I must consider Kenny's alternative suggestion.

Kenny contrasts the logic of satisfaction, not with a logic of validity, but with what he calls a 'logic of satisfactoriness', in which the preserved value (the analogue of truth in ordinary logic) is satisfactoriness relative to a given set of wishes or purposes. He thinks that the latter is the principal 'logic of imperatives', and his article is mainly occupied with its exposition and defence. He thinks that such a logic will have determinate rules, and that they will be the mirror-image of the rules of ordinary assertoric logic (and thus, also, of the rules of the logic of satisfaction). That is to say, if in ordinary assertoric logic a certain premiss entails a certain conclusion, and if we then convert each of these propositions into the imperative mood and reverse their order, so that what was the premiss becomes the conclusion and vice versa, we shall have a valid inference in the logic of satisfactoriness. For example, since there is a valid inference from 'You will do a and you will do b' to 'You will do a', there is a valid inference in the logic of satisfactoriness from 'Do a' to 'Do a and do b'.

This example is, of course, paradoxical, and critics have not been slow to say so. However, Kenny has been supported by Professor Geach; and his logic of satisfactoriness has some apparent merits. It is claimed for it that it makes *invalid* some inferences in the imperative mood which would be valid if imperative logic were isomorphic with assertoric logic, but which many people have found paradoxical – for example, the inference from 'Post the letter' to 'Post the letter or burn it' (an example, now famous, which was first used by Ross in the article referred to). Since, however, I have my own solution of this paradox, which seems to me more plausible than Kenny's (see pp. 25 ff. of this volume), I will say no more about it here. It is also claimed for the logic of satisfactoriness that it makes valid some of Aristotle's examples which would not be valid if practical inferences were governed by rules isomorphic with those of assertoric logic, but which seem sensible enough. These inferences are those, precisely, in which (as noted above) the reasoning is to a sufficient condition of fulfilling the premisses. This, as we shall see, gives us the key to an understanding of the whole matter.

Nevertheless, it is hardly surprising that the paradoxes of the logic of satisfactoriness have made it unacceptable to many. Two typical examples are the inferences (both of which are valid in this logic) from 'Reserve me a room in the best hotel in town' to 'Reserve me all the rooms in all the hotels in town', and from 'Open the door' to 'Open the door and smash the window' (Kenny's example). Professor André Gombay has shed a lot of light on these paradoxes (*Analysis*, XXVII 5, 1966–7), and I shall not discuss them at length. Kenny can reply to his critics that, indubitably, if the premisses of these inferences are satisfactory (as he puts it) relative to a set of wishes or purposes (in the sense that the fulfilment of the premisses would fulfil the wishes or purposes), then the conclusions would likewise fulfil them, and are therefore (in the same sense) satisfactory relative to them. It is significant, as we shall see, that what are here in question are the *sufficient* conditions for fulfilling commands, purposes or wishes.

Kenny can also, as he has pointed out to me, reply to another criticism which was suggested to me (though not in precisely this form) by Mr R. F. Stalley. According to the logic of satisfactoriness, I can deduce the command 'Shut the door' from the command 'Shut the door or shut the window'. But in the case of ordinary valid logical inferences, he who assents to the premisses is *compelled* not to dissent from the conclusion, on pain of logical inconsistency. It might be suggested that with the present inference this rule does not hold. I can without any inconsistency agree to shut the door or shut the window, and then refuse to shut the door, provided that I shut the window. So, it might be suggested, even if inferences in the logic of satisfactoriness do preserve satisfactoriness in Kenny's sense (relative to a set of purposes), they lack a feature which all ordinary logics have, namely the prohibition on dissenting from the conclusion of a valid inference whose premisses one has accepted.

Kenny can reply to this that to assent, in the logic of satisfactoriness, is to find what is assented to satisfactory for a given purpose; and if i_2 can be derived from i_1 in the logic of satisfactoriness, then it would be inconsistent to assent (in this sense) to i_1 and dissent from i_2. But this involves interpeting 'assent' in a rather special way, just as the answer to the previous objection involves interpreting 'satisfactory' in a rather special way. Normally, if we assent to a command (e.g. by saying 'Yes, shut the door' after someone has said 'Shut the door' to a third party, or by saying 'Yes, I'll shut the door', if it was addressed to oneself), we are taken to be, in the first case, commanding that that command be executed, and in the second, agreeing to execute it. But in the sense of 'assent' in which these are examples of assenting, it is not true that the person who assents to the premisses of a valid inference in the logic of satisfactoriness is compelled, on pain of inconsistency, not to dissent from the conclusion. To dissent from a command is to assent to its contradictory; and if I assent to the command 'Shut the door or shut the window' but say 'Don't shut the door' (thereby dissenting from the command 'Shut the door') I am guilty of no logical inconsistency (*pace* Prof. B. A. O. Williams; see my discussion on pp. 25 ff. of this volume). And I can, also without inconsistency, agree to shut the door or shut the window, but refuse to shut the door. Thus, although Kenny can answer this objection, he can do so only by taking 'assent' in a rather special sense.

It will be noticed that Kenny's pair of logics corresponds very closely in its properties with the two kinds of reasoning that I described at the beginning of this paper – reasoning to necessary and to sufficient conditions. This is hardly surprising, since I was led to pay attention to my pair by reflection on Kenny's article and on the many private discussions I have profitably engaged in with him. On the one hand we have a logic (his and Ross's 'logic of satisfaction', and my 'reasoning to necessary conditions') which is isomorphic with ordinary assertoric logic – for it is evident that if p entails q in the ordinary sense of 'entail', q states a necessary condition for the truth or the fulfilment of p. On the other hand we have a logic (Kenny's 'logic of satisfactoriness' and my 'reasoning to sufficient conditions') which is isomorphic with the mirror-image of ordinary assertoric logic – for if p entails q in the ordinary sense of 'entail', p states a sufficient condition for the truth or fulfilment of q. Let us suppose that two imperatives i_1 and i_2 are so related logically that 'i_1 is satisfied' entails 'i_2 is satisfied'. It will then be the case that a person who is given i_1, and is reasoning how to fulfil it, can infer that to satisfy i_2 would be a necessary condition of satisfying i_1. And it will also be the case that a person who is given i_2, and is reasoning how to fulfil it, can infer that to satisfy i_1, would be a sufficient condition of satisfying i_2.

Thus, if I am told to sing a song, and know that the Horst Wessel song is a song, I can reason that to sing the Horst Wessel would be *a way* (i.e. a sufficient condition) of fulfilling the original command. And if I am asked to give a performance of *Die schöne Müllerin*, I can reason that, since a performance of this song-cycle would be incomplete without an accompanist, I *must* get an accompanist in order to comply with this request – it is a necessary condition of doing so. Examination of Aristotle's examples makes clear that they are all perfectly good examples of one or the other of these sorts of reasoning; the pity is that he did not distinguish them. And it is also a pity that Kenny put his essentially correct view in the highly misleading way that he did; for he not only generated needless paradoxes, but also created the impression that he had discovered a type of 'imperative logic' which was radically different from ordinary logic – whereas in fact the logic of reasoning to sufficient conditions is a well-established application of ordinary logic.

The paradoxes are easily disposed of. They vanish, once we see that a man who is told to open the door, and reasons that a *sufficient* condition of doing this would be to open the door and smash the window, is reasoning with perfect logic. If he then proceeds to open the door and smash the window, what we can blame him for is doing something that was not *necessary* in order to fulfil the original command, and which was objectionable on other grounds. He could be convicted of logical error only if he mistakenly supposed that opening the door and smashing the window was a *necessary* condition of fulfilling the command to open the door. And the other paradoxes can be dealt with similarly.

The two most interesting questions which now arise are: (1) Are we left with anything that is peculiar to practical inferences? (2) Is it necessary any longer to speak of practical inferences at all? I shall answer that there is nothing here peculiar to practical inferences, but that it is harmless, and even useful, to speak of practical inferences in a rather modest sense.

The logic of necessary and sufficient conditions is a well-worn application of ordinary logic; and so it is not necessary to claim that Kenny's logic of satisfactoriness, when redescribed as a logic of sufficient conditions, introduces any element peculiar to imperatives or practical inferences. It might be the case (though, as we shall see, it is not) that in practical reasoning we always inferred sufficient conditions, and in theoretical reasoning never. In actual fact, the most that can be said is that reasoning to sufficient conditions is somewhat commoner (because more commonly useful) in practical thought than in theoretical.

We do, however, sometimes reason to necessary conditions in practical contexts (as in the 'All men, march' example, and still more often when we are obeying a universal *prohibition*). And we do sometimes reason to sufficient conditions in theoretical contexts. An interesting case is where we are trying to *explain* something. We are, for example, told that Harry is late, and suggest, as an explanation of this, that his train is late. We may say 'Harry is late; but the 10.45 being late is something that would make Harry late; so (perhaps) the 10.45 is late'. What we have done is, given the information that Harry is late, to look for some true proposition whose truth is a sufficient condition (in this case a causally sufficient condition, given certain obvious additional assumptions) of his being late. That is what 'an explanation' often means. This inference is isomorphic with one which a powerful and unscrupulous railway official might perform, if he had resolved (or been told) to make Harry late: he might say 'I am to make Harry late; but to make the 10.45 late would be a way of making Harry late; so (perhaps) I'll make the 10.45 late'. Both inferences are of the form 'p; but if q then p; so (perhaps) q'. I write 'perhaps' in the conclusion in both cases because in neither case would the inferrer be guilty of any logical inconsistency if he assented to 'p' and to 'if q then p', but dissented from 'q'. The affirmation of 'q' is a possible, but perhaps not the only possible (not a necessary) solution to the problem posed by the affirmation of 'p'. In both cases *some particular* solution (e.g. this one) has to be plumped for; and the plumping is no part of the inference, but is done on extraneous considerations. However, the inference sets the stage for the plumping – it presents us with a possibility, and other such inferences may present us with other possibilities, and we then decide between them.

The situation is very different when we reason to a necessary condition. The reasoning is then compelling, and there is no decision left to be made, unless we are going to renege on one of the premisses.

Secondly, to what extent is it useful and to what extent is it misleading to speak of practical inferences? A possible way of discussing this question is to ask how much of what I have said could be accepted by someone who, like Ross when he wrote his 'Imperatives and Logic' article, was sceptical about the admission of any special sort of reasoning called 'Practical Reasoning'. I hope that I am not being too sanguine in suggesting that he might have accepted all of it, without admitting anything damaging to his main standpoint. For I have not admitted any inferences which could not be represented as perfectly straightforward uses of ordinary assertoric logic. For example, the man who, having been told to sing a song, reasons that singing the Horst Wessel song would be a way of executing this command, could be represented as inferring from the statement 'If I sing the Horst Wessel song, I shall be singing a song' in conjunction with the statement 'I have been told to sing a song', the conclusion 'If I sing the Horst Wessel song, I shall be doing the thing that I have been told to do'. It might be alleged that this purely assertoric inference is the only logical part of what he does; his decision, having done this reasoning, to sing the Horst Wessel song is not a conclusion but, as I have called it, a decision.

But to say this would be misleading. In the first place, it leaves out of account the other kind of reasoning described, that to a necessary condition. Surely the man who, having been told never to smoke, refrains from smoking now has not, once he has assented to the original prohibition, had to make any decision at all; it has been made for him by the logic. But even in the case of reasoning to sufficient conditions, to say that the *inference* is purely assertoric, and that logic has nothing to do with the *decision*, would be wrong. On the contrary, the man who could not do the piece of inferring about the Horst Wessel song set out in the preceding paragraph, and other similar ones, would not know what to do in order to execute any commands given him, other than logically simple ones. In this sense, logic is essential to practice. And, moreover, it is because of the logical properties of the words in the imperative sentence 'Sing a song' that the man can reason about what would be a way of executing the command. In this sense imperatives have a logic.

This explains the necessity for some device to relate each imperative sentence to its corresponding indicative (e.g. 'Shut the door' to 'You are going to shut the door'). One such device is the 'phrastic-tropic (or neustic)' formulation which I adopted in *The Language of Morals*. Another is to say that all imperatives can be rewritten 'Let it be made the case that . . .' followed by a complete indicative sentence. The two devices are very similar in their formal consequences, and this is hardly the place to discuss their relative merits. Ross, in the article referred to, speaks of a 'theme of demand', which may, I think, be interpreted either as a phrastic or as an indicative sentence governed by an imperative operator. It is obvious that without some device of this general sort, we should have no means of knowing *what* assertion was equivalent to the assertion that the command 'Open the door' is (or will be) satisfied. We know this, only because we can unhesitatingly convert this imperative into its corresponding indicative 'You are going to open the door'; and this we can do, only because we can, as it were, extract from the imperative its 'theme of demand' and discard the imperative tropic.

Thus imperatives come within logic in the sense that logical operations upon them are possible, because of the logical properties which they have. And these logical properties include this very important one, that there can be inconsistencies between commands. This notion can be defined for commands as follows: if two commands are such that they logically cannot both be satisfied (i.e. if the statements that they are satisfied are mutually inconsistent), then the commands are mutually inconsistent. Thus there is imposed on us, if we are going to avoid logical inconsistency, the necessity of making the conjunction of our commands (and by parity of reasoning our intentions) consistent. If we include statements as well as commands in the conjunction, the whole lot has to be mutually consistent; but the question of the logical relations between imperatives and indicatives (mixed inferences, derivations of indicatives from imperatives and vice versa, and the like) is too large and productive of difficulties to be discussed in this article.

It might be suggested that the basic principle of the logic of imperatives is that one is not allowed, on pain of inconsistency, to issue a set of commands which logically cannot be conjointly satisfied. The logic generated by this principle would be Ross's and Kenny's 'logic of satisfaction', which, as we have seen, is isomorphic with ordinary assertoric logic, and also with my 'reasoning to necessary conditions'. It would legitimate inferences such as that from 'Do *a* and do *b*' to 'Do *a*'; it would do this because the person who issues the first command and then issues the contradictory of the second is guilty of an inconsistency, in just the same way as the person who makes the statement 'You are going to do *a* and you are going to do *b*', and then makes a statement which is the contradictory of 'You are going to do *a*', is guilty of an inconsistency. It is fortunately not necessary, for this argument, to establish what *is* the contradictory of the command 'Do *a*' – a question on which Mr Bergström and I have recently been in dispute in the pages of *Mind* (1970).

Another way of putting this point is to say that the logic of imperatives tells us what commands we cannot in consistency dissent from, if we have issued a certain set of commands (and, if statements be included, statements). It is when the point is put in this way that the inference from 'Post the letter' to 'Post the letter or burn it' seems, prima facie, paradoxical; but I have tried to show in my article referred to that the paradox, and others like it, can be generated just as easily in the case of assertoric inferences which nearly everyone accepts, and that it is no real paradox. It is in fact correct to say that if a man issues the command 'Post the letter', he cannot consistently dissent from the command 'Post the letter or burn it'. For to dissent from a command is to assent to its contradictory; and the contradictory of '(Either) post the letter or burn it' certainly *seems* (*pace* Bergström) to be 'Do not either post the letter or burn it'; and this clearly cannot with consistency be assented to by a man who has issued the command 'Post the letter'. However, it is not my intention to continue this particular controversy in the present article.

From the 'logic of satisfaction', as so described, we can develop my 'reasoning to sufficient conditions', and Kenny's 'logic of satisfactoriness', in exactly the same way as the logic of sufficient conditions is developed from ordinary assertoric logic; the 'mirror image' effect will of course appear in both cases. As we have seen, there will be no paradoxes provided that we understand what we are up to.

Lastly, we may ask what happens in this scheme to Ross's 'logic of (subjective) validity' – the logic which proceeds from premisses of the form 'i_1 is demanded or accepted by a certain person' to conclusions of the form 'i_2 is demanded or accepted by that person'. Ross contended, in effect, that all so-called inferences in this logic were invalid except some uninteresting ones in which i_1 and i_2 were verbally identical. This was because, if they are not identical, no inference from 'A demands i_1' to 'A demands i_2' can validly be drawn without an additional contingent premiss about the commander, A. At one point, speaking of the inference from 'A demands i_1' to 'A does not demand the contradictory of i_1', Ross says that the inference would be valid if we were given the additional premiss that 'within the system in question there are no duties telling us to perform incompatible actions' (p. 40). He goes on to say that this 'is self-evident to a practical attitude of mind'.

I want now to suggest that in saying this Ross has (perhaps unintentionally) provided us with the means of understanding how practical reasoning is possible. For in practical, as in theoretical, reasoning, it is a presupposition that the reasoner does not commit inconsistencies. That this is a presupposition in both cases can easily be seen. If I assent to 'p and q' (where 'p' and 'q' are assertions), I am bound not to dissent from 'p', *if and only if I am to avoid inconsistency*. Of course, if (like Walt Whitman) I do not care about inconsistency, I can say 'p and q and not p' with equanimity. In the same way, I am bound, having said 'Do *a* and do *b*', not to say the contradictory of 'Do *a*', if and only if I am to avoid inconsistency. So the necessary and sufficient condition of being bound by the rules of logic is the same in both cases, viz. that we should have the intention of playing the logical game, i.e. of talking non-self-contradictorily. That we have this intention is certainly, as Ross implies, a contingent fact; but it is not contingent that unless we have it, we are not doing logic, and are not bound by its rules. If, in the practical case, a person *is* seeking to avoid inconsistency, he must not assent to (which includes both issuing and accepting) commands which logically cannot conjointly be satisfied. It is also the case that inconsistencies *are* inconsistencies, whether or not their utterer cares about this.

It must be noted that it is the reasoner that is here in question, and not anybody else. In both assertoric and imperative logic a conclusion follows from a premiss if a person cannot without inconsistency assent to the second and dissent from the first. Provided that I, the reasoner, abide by the rules of this game, it does not matter what inconsistencies anybody else may commit. If somebody gives me a command, I may be quite unable to predict what other commands, consistent or inconsistent with the first one, he may give. In thinking this, Ross is absolutely right. But it is possible for me to reason that if I, or if anybody else, assents to the command he has given me, we cannot, *if we are going to be consistent*, dissent from the commands which follow from it. And this is all that is required for an imperative logic. Imperative logic is about what can be commanded by a consistent commander, just as assertoric logic is about what can be stated by a maker of consistent statements. Such an imperative logic has no need of an objective validity of *commands*; whether its *inferences* are any less objectively valid than those of assertoric logic, I leave to be decided by anybody who is surer than I am what is meant by 'objective'.

I have discussed in this paper only some of the insights to be found in Alf Ross's article of twenty-four years ago. That he still has much to teach us on this subject is clear from his recent book *Directives and Norms*; but I must leave the discussion of this interesting book for a forthcoming review in *Mind*.[1]

[1] *Mind*, LXXVIII (1969) 464.

5 Meaning and Speech Acts

1. *Introduction*

A controversy has been brewing up for some time now between those who want to explain the meanings of certain words in terms of the speech acts which those words (or sentences containing them) are standardly used to perform, and those who say that this is a mistake. Let us call these two parties the performers and the critics. I have myself, in my treatment of 'good', put on one of the performances which is criticised; and Professor Strawson, in his account of 'true', has put on another.[1] Professor Searle appears by turns as one of the most interesting performers and as one of the most trenchant critics. For he says, in general, in his recent excellent book, *Speech Acts*:

> A study of the meaning of sentences is not in principle distinct from a study of speech acts. Properly construed, they are the same study. Since every meaningful sentence in virtue of its meaning can be used to perform a particular speech act (or range of speech acts), and since every possible speech act can in principle be given an exact formulation in a sentence or sentences (assuming an appropriate context of utterance), the study of the meanings of sentences and the study of speech acts are not two independent studies but one study from two different points of view (p. 18);

and in an article, with which I agree almost entirely, he attacks the view (attributed perhaps wrongly to Austin) that meaning is wholly distinct from illocutionary force.[2] And in particular he convincingly analyses the word 'promise' in terms of the speech act of promising,[3] and analyses referring expressions in terms of the speech act of referring.[4] But on the other hand he

[1] See his articles in *Truth*, ed. G. Pitcher.
[2] *Philosophical Review*, LXXVII (1968).
[3] *Speech Acts*, chap. 3; *Philosophical Review*, LXXIII (1964) 44 f.
[4] *Speech Acts*, chap. 4.

First published in *Philosophical Review*, LXXIX (1970).

severely criticises those who would treat 'good' in a similar way.[1]

Searle's book is a welcome sign of the growing interest in this aspect of meaning theory. When we understand more about it, we shall know what has put us at cross-purposes; and it is as a contribution to such an understanding, rather than merely as a defence of my own views, that this article is intended.

The performers put forward theories of the following general type: they claim that the meaning of a certain word can be explained, or partly explained, by saying that, when incorporated in an appropriate sentence in an appropriate place, it gives to that whole sentence the property that an utterance of it would be, in the appropriate context, a performance of a certain kind of speech act. This is the same as to say that the utterance would have, in Austin's term, a certain illocutionary force; and it is the same as to say, with Professor Alston, that the sentence has a certain illocutionary-act potential.[2] Thus, to take Searle's relatively uncontroversial example, the incorporation of the word 'promise' in that particular place in the sentence (that particular sentence) 'I promise to pay you $5 tomorrow' gives to that whole sentence the property that an utterance of it would be, in an appropriate context, a performance of the speech act of promising to pay the person addressed $5 on the day following the utterance; and, it is claimed, to say this is to say something (not necessarily everything) about the meaning of the word 'promise'. This is intended as a general characterisation of the type of theory, not as a statement of Searle's own views, for which his book can be consulted.

To proceed to a more controversial example with which I shall be most concerned: it has been claimed that the incorporation of the word 'good' in the sentence 'That is a good movie' gives to the whole sentence the property that an utterance of it would be, in an appropriate context, a performance of the speech act of commending the film in question; and that to say this is to say something (but not necessarily everything) about the meaning of the word 'good'. Naturally, it has to be further explained what the speech act of commending is; but this I shall not attempt in this paper. The above claim is to be carefully distinguished from the claim that the sentence 'That is a

[1] *Philosophical Review*, LXXI (1962); *Speech Acts*, chap. 6.2.
[2] *Philosophy of Language*, chap. 2.

good movie' means the same as the explicit performative 'I (hereby) commend that as a movie', to which, as we shall see, there is a powerful objection. It is also to be distinguished from the claim that 'That is a good movie' means the same as the report 'I do, as a matter of fact, commend that as a movie'. I do not know whether anybody has ever made either of these claims.

The criticism which the critics put forward can come in bolder or in less bold forms, which must be distinguished. I leave it to the reader to examine the writings of the critics and see how bold each of them is (Searle's views on 'promise' put him into the less bold class). In the bolder form, the criticism would say that illocutionary force is something different from meaning, and that therefore no account of the illocutionary force of an utterance tells us anything about the meaning of the utterance or of any word used in it. A less bold form of the criticism would be this: although there are certain words whose meaning can be explained, or partly explained, by giving the illocutionary force of utterances in which they occur ('promise' would be an example), this is not the case with certain other words which have figured in well-known theories (for example, that about 'good' just mentioned).

I shall not attempt in this paper to solve all the manifold problems of speech-act theory; nor even to deal with all the critics' arguments. I shall deal only with what has appeared to many to be their strongest one. This runs as follows. The words in question occur not only in affirmative, categorical, indicative sentences, but also in negative sentences, interrogative sentences, and subordinate clauses of all kinds, including especially conditional clauses. In all these other contexts, it is false to say that the man who utters the sentence containing the word is thereby performing the speech act which he *is* performing when he utters an affirmative categorical indicative sentence containing the word. Thus, although it may be admitted for the sake of argument that when I say 'That was a good movie' I am commending the movie, I am not commending it (nor is anybody else) when I say 'That is not a good movie' or 'Is that a good movie?' or 'If it is a good movie, it will make a lot of money'. But, the critics go on, an explanation of the meaning of a word must take into account all these contexts, and make it possible for it to have the same meaning in them all. Otherwise, for example, the man who says 'It is not a good movie' will not be denying what the man who says 'It is a good movie' is affirming; the statement 'It is a good movie' will not be an answer to the question 'Is it a good movie?' (for the questioner and answerer will be at cross-purposes); and the inference from 'If it is a good movie, it will make a lot of money' in conjunction with 'It is a good movie' to 'It will make a lot of money' will suffer from a fallacy of equivocation. These absurd results, say the critics, can be avoided only if we insist that an explanation of the meaning of a word must allow it the same meaning in all such syntactical transformations. But this, it is alleged, the performers do not do.

A critic might make use of all the instances I have cited. But most critics lay more weight on the conditional case – no doubt because they think it the hardest for a performer to deal with. I shall reverse this tactic, and start with the negative and interrogative cases, in which the point I wish to make against the critics can be expounded most clearly. And I shall attempt first to refute the bolder critics (those who think that illocutionary force is altogether different from meaning), and after that assail the timider critics (who think that sometimes meaning can be explained partly in terms of illocutionary force, but not in the case of 'good').

2. *Questions and Negations*

I shall use two examples of illocutionary-force indicating devices. The first is the word 'promise' already mentioned. The second is the sign of indicative or imperative mood which occurs regularly in natural languages and is, as we shall briefly note, a necessity for logic. Both these linguistic elements, in their central or standard uses, act as signs that a certain kind of speech act is being performed. In the affirmative categorical, the occurrence of 'I promise' indicates that the speaker is promising. Likewise, the fact that, in an utterance like 'The cat is on the mat', the verb is indicative tells us, in the absence of certain contextual counter-indications, that the speaker is performing one of the genus of speech acts which we may call 'assertions'. Species of this genus are: statements, declarations, guesses, and so forth. Although this is not the place to characterise either the species or the genus as accurately as they need, it is very important that there are both species and genera of speech acts; some weak arguments have recently been founded on the neglect of this fact.[1]

Would someone who did not know that the man who said 'I promise' was promising, or that the man who said 'The cat is on the mat' was making an assertion, be said to know the meaning of these words? The answer seems to be plainly that he would not. The Latin words '*i*' ('go', imperative) and '*ibis*' ('you will go', future indicative) clearly have different meanings. Any complete explanation of the meaning of a verb occurring in a sentence must explain the meaning of its mood (in the sense in which indicative and imperative are moods) as well as, for example, its tense, person, voice, and so forth; and it is hard to see how this could be done otherwise than by specifying the kind of speech act to which that mood is assigned by the conventions which constitute our language. To be in a certain mood is to be assigned to the performance of a certain genus of speech acts. And analogously, to say what we mean by 'I promise' we have to make clear that in uttering it (in the appropriate context) we are promising and, of course, make clear also what the speech act of promising is.[2]

Having given this explanation of 'I promise' in the sentence 'I promise to pay you $5 tomorrow', how do we go on to explain the meanings of utterances like 'Do you promise to pay me $5 tomorrow?' and 'I do not promise to pay you $5 tomorrow'? Here there is a trap to be avoided. Some occurrences of the verb 'promise' which are not themselves performances of the speech act of promising are to be explained as reports or predictions or in general statements that such an act has been or is being or will be performed. For example, if I am writing something on a piece of paper, and you ask me what I am doing, I may say 'I am just promising to pay Jones $5 tomorrow'. In what follows, we must put aside, entirely, such second-order statements about speech acts, since they are quite irrelevant to the question we are discussing and can only be a source of confusion – as, indeed, they have often been. It would be a serious mistake to suppose that 'Do you promise to pay me $5 tomor-

[1] See, e.g., my review of G. J. Warnock, *Contemporary Moral Philosophy*, in *Mind*, LXXVII (1968) 436.

[2] Cf. Searle, 'How to Derive "Ought" from "Is"', *Philosophical Review*, LXXIII (1964) 44 f.; and *Speech Acts*, pp. 20 f., 178 f.

row?' means the same as 'Are you promising to pay me $5 tomorrow?' (except as the latter expression is used in the dialect of Damon Runyon). The former admits of the answer 'Yes, I promise', which is a promise; the latter admits of the answer 'Yes, I am promising', which is not a promise but a report of a promise.

Even the words 'I promise' are sometimes used to make not promises but statements about promises. For example, if asked 'What do you do if you can't pay the money that you owe?', I may answer 'I promise to pay tomorrow'. This use also must be carefully put aside.

We are concerned, then, with the question 'Do you promise?' which admits a promise as an answer, and with the negation 'I do not promise' which is the negation (in some sense) of a promise. It has to be asked how, in the light of these examples, it can be claimed – as it is tempting to claim, and as at any rate one of the critics, Searle, does claim – both that the meaning of 'I promise' can be explained by explaining the speech act which is performed in utterances containing it,[1] and that 'Any analysis of the meaning of a word (or morpheme) must be consistent with the fact that the same word (or morpheme) can mean the same thing in all the grammatically different kinds of sentences in which it can occur'.[2] For if the meaning of 'I promise' is to be explained by saying that it is the phrase we use for performing the speech act of promising, as maintained in the first thesis, then, by the second thesis, we ought to be performing the speech act of promising when we say 'Do you promise?' or 'I do not promise'; but we are not. Yet both theses seem to have a lot to be said for them; so we must try to find a way of interpreting them which will allow us to hold both of them in the face of such apparent counter-examples.

The clue to the interpretation lies in a phrase used by Searle: he says that the speech act in question is sometimes not actually performed in the utterance of the word, but is 'in the offing'.[3] He unfortunately does not sufficiently distinguish between the different ways in which a speech act can be 'in the offing', and confines his attention to cases in which the act is reported, and the like (the cases which we have just put aside). In his latest account of the matter,[4] he says, correctly, that performers

[1] *Speech Acts*, pp. 57–61.   [2] Ibid., p. 137.
[3] *Philosophical Review*, LXXI (1962) 425.   [4] *Speech Acts*, p. 138.

'were thus not committed to the view that every literal utterance of W is a performance of act A, but rather that utterances which are not performances of the act have to be explained in terms of utterances which are'. But in suggesting possible explanations of this sort, he considers only cases in which W (the word whose meaning is being explained) occurs as part of a report of a speech act or in some closely related manner. For example, he speaks of cases where the act is reported in the past ('He promised'), cases where it is 'hypothesised' ('If he promises . . .'); and adds 'etc.' He might have added cases where it is denied that the act took place or will take place or is taking place (negations of reports or predictions) and cases where it is asked whether it took place, and so forth (questions requiring as answers reports, and so forth, or their negations). But having mentioned this class of cases, which we have ourselves put aside as irrelevant, he passes on without considering the cases which we have just mentioned – namely, those in which what is negated is not a report of a promise but a promise, and those in which the question expects as answer not a report, but either a promise or the negation of a promise. In these, the speech act is in the offing in a different way; but all the same it is possible for the performer to explain the meaning of the word 'promise', in this syntactical context, in terms of it, as we shall see. The trouble for Searle is that the type of explanation, once understood, can be extended to cover 'good' as well as 'promise', as we shall also see.

How then can we explain the meaning of 'Do you promise?' and 'I do not promise'? We can do it indirectly, by first explaining the meaning of 'I promise' as the phrase we use for promising, and then applying to this result what we already know about the meanings of the interrogative sentence form or sentence frame, and likewise the negative. I shall not actually, in this paper, try to explain the meaning of 'I promise' (Searle has done it fairly successfully), or of the negative sentence form (which has been the subject of much discussion and is still obscure). But something needs to be said about the type of interrogative sentence form exemplified by 'Do you promise?' The simplest explanation of this kind of interrogative sentence form that I have been able to think of is that typified by many questionnaires and by multiple-choice examinations. A question (of the type we are considering) is an invitation or request, or perhaps on occasions even an order, to make just one out of a number of suggested assertions. Thus a questionnaire may begin 'Check as applicable (or appropriate)', and contain a lot of sentences like

    I am married ☐
    I am not married ☐

This is to offer the answerer an opportunity (indeed, positively to tell him) to make either the assertion that he is married, or the assertion that he is not married. Note that this invitation does not imply a permission to make either of these assertions at will; before he can decide which to make, the answerer has to consider which he is willing to make, which will, if he is a truthful person, depend on which is true. In passing, we may notice that the other kind of question, that prefaced by words like 'Who' or 'How', could be analysed as an invitation, and so forth, to fill in a constant in place of a variable in a propositional function. Searle is no doubt aware of all this,[1] and the point is not a new one.[2]

If we apply the same method to the question 'Do you promise to pay me $5 tomorrow?', we get the pair of promise expressions (instead of assertion expressions)

    I promise to pay you $5 tomorrow ☐
    I do not promise to pay you $5 tomorrow ☐

similarly prefaced by some such request as 'Check as appropriate'. What answer is given will be, as before, determined by whether the answerer is willing to make the promise or not (though, of course, the affirmative answer is not a *statement that* he is willing, nor the negative answer a *statement that* he is not, any more than in the previous case the answers were statements that the answerer was willing to make the affirmative or negative assertions; just as those answers were assertions, so these are a promise and an act of declining to promise). The type of negation is, however, different in the two cases, as we shall shortly see.

We may observe in passing that the check or tick which the

---

[1] Cf. *Speech Acts*, p. 69.
[2] See my article in *Mind*, LVIII (1949) 24 (above p. 5), in which I was not conscious of being original.

answerer puts in the appropriate box, coupled with his signature of the entire document, constitutes a very important element in language, to which I shall come back near the end of this paper, and call the 'sign of subscription' or 'neustic'. The left-hand (vertical) stroke of Frege's 'assertion-sign' had this role. Wittgenstein's dismissal of Frege's sign as 'logically meaningless'[1] was perhaps too hasty. But I must leave a full discussion of these 'subatomic particles' of logic, however tempting, for another occasion. The sign of subscription, or neustic, is to be distinguished from the sign of mood, or, as I shall be calling it, the tropic; and both are to be distinguished from the term used above, 'sentence form', which is a much wider notion (see below).

We have thus explained the meaning of 'Do you promise to pay me $5 tomorrow?' in two stages. First, we explained the meaning of 'I promise' by saying that it was the phrase used to perform a certain speech act; then, we gave a general explanation of the interrogative sentence form. The speech act of promising is not being performed by the man who utters the interrogative; but once we understand the meaning of the categorical affirmative 'I promise' in terms of the speech act which its utterer performs, and understand the meaning of the interrogative sentence form, we are in a position to put the two together and understand the meaning of the interrogative 'Do you promise?'

What about the negative 'I do not promise'? It would be out of place here, as I have said, to attempt a general explanation of what negation is – a much more difficult matter than interrogation. But there is a complication which must be noted. There are two kinds of negation (at least). They are commonly called 'internal' and 'external' negation. The internal negation of 'I promise to pay you before the end of the tax year' is 'I promise not to pay you before the end of the tax year'. The external negation of the same promise is 'I do not promise to pay you before the end of the tax year'. Nearly all speech acts, including assertions, can be negated in these two ways. The internal negation of 'The cat is on the mat' is, of course, 'The cat is not on the mat'. Its external negation is normally expressed by the use of a negated explicit performative: 'I don't say that the cat is on the mat', but it is arguable that one use of the

[1] *Tractatus*, 4.442; *Investigations*, par. 21 ff.

sentence 'The cat may not be on the mat' is to express this same external negation.[1]

A similar account is to be given in all these cases of how we get from the meaning of the categorical affirmative to the meaning of the negative of either sort. It is the same as before: we know the meaning of the categorical affirmative 'I promise to pay' (by reference to the speech act of promising); we know the two negative sentence forms; thus we apply these sentence forms to the categorical affirmative 'I promise to pay', and get the two kinds of negative 'I do not promise to pay' and 'I promise not to pay'. And thus we know that the man who utters the first is (explicitly) refraining from performing the speech act in question, whereas the man who utters the second is performing the speech act (of the same type – that is, a promise) whose content is the negation of the content of 'I promise to pay'.

The same thing happens with mood signs. We cannot know the meaning of the indicative sentence 'The cat is on the mat' unless we know, among other things, the meaning attached to the indicative mood of the verb 'is'. We know this when we know that it is the mood we use for performing the speech act of asserting, and not, for example, commanding. Then, if someone says 'Is the cat on the mat?', we know the meaning of this because we know, in addition, the meaning of the interrogative sentence form. We know, that is to say, that the person who says this is performing the speech act of asking us to perform either the speech act of asserting that the cat is on the mat, or the speech act of asserting its internal negation (as appropriate), but not both. That the alternative to affirmation is internal negation in this case, and not external negation as in the case of 'Do you promise?', is apparent from the form of the questions: 'Do you promise?' uses the explicit performative verb, and thus invites the alternative answers (also using it) 'I promise' or 'I do not promise'; 'Is the cat on the mat?' is the interrogative transform of what Austin might have called the 'primary', as opposed to 'explicit', assertion, and therefore admits as answers either the primary assertion ('The cat is on the mat') or its negation, which is normally internal. 'I don't say that it is' would hardly be an *answer* to 'Is the cat on the mat?'

[1] See my article above, p. 38. A similar suggestion has been made by the linguists J. Boyd and J. P. Thorne in a paper, 'The Semantics of Modal Verbs', *Journal of Linguistics*, v (1969) 57.

We know the meaning of the negatives of both kinds because we know the meanings of their corresponding affirmatives (which involves knowing about the speech acts which they are standardly used to perform) and know also the use of the different negative sentence forms. I have been assuming with Frege[1] that both internal negations and their corresponding affirmations are properly treated as assertions; the difference is that in the negation what is asserted is negative. Since I have made this assumption, a critic might object that my answer to him, in the case of internal negation, misfires. He might admit that in the affirmative 'The cat is on the mat' the word 'is' has to have its mood explained by saying that it is the mood used for assertion. But he might claim that since in the internal negation, too, an assertion is made (a negative one), there is no objection here, on any view, to treating 'is' and its mood sign as meaning the same in both cases. Therefore, he might claim, I cannot use this example as a parallel to what happens in the case of 'good'; for there, on my view, the affirmative expresses a commendation whereas the negative does not (the speech acts differ), but in the case of 'The cat is on the mat' and its internal negation, since both are assertions, there is no difference in speech act. But this objection misses the point. To explain the meaning of 'The cat is on the mat' I have to explain not merely that it is an assertion, but *what* assertion it is. An explanation of the meaning even of the internal negation, therefore, has to explain how, once we know the meaning of 'The cat is on the mat' (by knowing that it is an assertion, and what assertion it is), we can go on to understand 'The cat is not on the mat', which is a *different* assertion, and therefore a *different* speech act, albeit one of the same assertoric kind.

However this may be, the interrogative examples and the example of the external negation of 'I promise' are sufficient to refute the *general* objection made by the bolder critics against explaining meaning in terms of speech acts. Not only have we shown (following and extending a move made by one of the less bold critics) that there are some expressions whose meaning has to be explained in terms of speech acts. We have also shown that when it has been so explained, the explanation can be extended to cover the meaning of utterances in which the speech act in question is not performed, provided that the utterance is

[1] 'Negation', in Geach and Black, p. 130.

generated by a transformation, whose form we understand, of the original speech act. The examples of negatives and interrogatives, therefore, provide no general objection to the general thesis that it is sometimes possible to explain meaning in terms of speech acts. The critics have to show that there is something special about 'good' or about commendation (or the other words and speech acts treated by the performers) which prevents the kind of explanation given above, and the kind of answer offered to the critics' objection, being used in these cases. It is not immediately obvious what this 'something special' could be. Why cannot we explain the meaning of the affirmative assertion 'That is a good movie' partly in terms of the speech act of commending the movie, and then explain the meaning of 'Is that a good movie?' and 'That is not a good movie' indirectly, as transformations of this, in an analogous manner to that used in the case of 'I promise' and the indicative mood sign? The question 'Is that a good movie?' seems to resolve itself quite naturally into an invitation to say either 'That is a good movie' (which is a commendation) or 'That is not a good movie' (which is the negation of a commendation). The same could be said about the indirect interrogative 'I wonder whether that is a good movie' (a type of example used by some critics); this is very similar in meaning to 'I ask myself, "Is that a good movie?"' Such cases present no extra difficulties beyond those associated with all cases of *oratio obliqua* – a form of speech whose logical character is still somewhat obscure.

Negation is more troublesome, because of its two varieties. It certainly looks as if 'That is not a good movie' were the *internal* negation of 'That is a good movie'; and, if that is so, certain consequences follow. It follows that we can do something with 'That is a good movie' which we cannot do with 'I (hereby) commend that movie' – namely, negate it internally. This provides the critics with an objection (similar to one which we shall put forward in more detail in the case of hypotheticals) to any performer who injudiciously claims that 'That is a good movie' is equivalent to 'I commend that movie'. But if the performer is content to put his thesis in the form that to say 'That is a good movie' is to commend it as a movie, it does not seem that this objection touches him. He has, no doubt, to admit that the commendation sentence 'That is a good movie' is like the assertion sentence 'That is a long movie' in this respect, that both can be internally negated; but does this do anything whatever to impugn the view that the former is, and the latter is not, a commendation sentence, and that this needs to be noted in any full explanation of its meaning? In other words, 'is a good movie' behaves grammatically like a predicate; but nobody need deny this, and it is perfectly consistent with the view that it is a predicate whose meaning has to be explained, in part, by mentioning the kind of speech act, commendation, which is standardly performed in uttering it.

3. *Hypotheticals*

A critic might accept what we have said about negations and questions, but demur to an extension of our defence to cover hypotheticals. Would he be justified in demurring? The key to this controversy lies in the question of how the hypothetical sentence form operates. It would be unfair to expect the performer to have a clear answer to this question to which nobody yet has a clear answer, any more than to the similar question about negation; he is to be criticised only if his thesis lands him in peculiar troubles which do not afflict those who disagree with him. I am going to be bold and offer a tentative (though not original) answer to the question of how hypotheticals work. To understand the 'If . . . then' form of sentence is to understand the place that it has in logic (to understand its logical properties). It is, in fact, to understand the operation of *modus ponens* and related inferences. If a man denies the validity of *modus ponens*, he must be using 'if' in a different way from most of us. As Professor Max Black says, 'Given a simple argument patently invalid, say of the form 'P, if P then Q, therefore not-Q', we can make no sense of the supposition that somebody might utter it, understand what he was saying, and mean what he seemed to be saying'.[1] We may notice in passing that this is the solution of Lewis Carroll's paradox about 'What the Tortoise Said to Achilles' (*Mind*, 1895). Achilles' correct reply to the Tortoise would have been that the Tortoise could not be using 'if' in the same way as most of us.

Suppose, then, that a man utters the hypothetical sentence 'If the cat is on the mat, it is purring'. As I pointed out earlier,

[1] *Philosophical Review*, LXXVII (1968) 177; cf. my *Language of Morals*, p. 25.

in order to understand the meaning of the affirmative categorical 'The cat is on the mat', we have to understand, among other things, the meaning of the mood of its verb, and to understand this is to know that this sentence, because its main verb is in this mood, is standardly used to perform the kind of speech act called 'making an assertion'. But in the conditional clause of the hypothetical no assertion is made, although the word 'is' occurs just the same. Ought not the critics to argue, therefore, that the use of this hypothetical plus the corresponding categorical 'The cat is on the mat' in a *modus ponens* would result in a fallacy of equivocation? For the argument is no different from that which they use against the performers. This same point has been made very succinctly and cogently by Mr Hinton.[1] How can the critics admit (as most of us do) the validity in general of *modus ponens*, without abandoning their argument against the performers' view of the meaning of 'good'? I can see only one way in which a critic might avoid this difficulty, and that is by denying what I have claimed earlier – namely, that in order to explain fully the meaning of 'is' we have to advert to the fact that it is in the indicative mood, and that this is the mood standardly used for the speech act of asserting. This, however, would be a difficult position to sustain in the light of the examples given earlier – and doubly difficult for philosophers like Searle who want, in general, to make an account of speech acts a very fundamental part of the theory of meaning.

To know the meaning of the whole sentence 'If the cat is on the mat, it is purring', we have to know (1) the meaning of the hypothetical sentence form, which we know if we know how to do *modus ponens*; (2) the meanings of the categoricals which have got encaged in this sentence form; and we know the latter if we know (*a*) that they are (when not encaged) used to make assertions and (*b*) what assertions they are used to make. And there is, so far as I can see, nothing to stop us knowing any of these things. Since we know them, we know how to handle the hypothetical assertion that has been made. We know, that is to say, that if we are in a position to affirm the categorical 'The cat is on the mat', we can go on to affirm the categorical 'It is purring'.

It is true, as in the case of negations, that both 'The cat is on the mat' and 'If the cat is on the mat it is purring' are used

[1] *Philosophical Books* (Leicester, 1964) pp. 22–4.

to make assertions, one categorical and one hypothetical. A critic might therefore claim that in this case there is no transition, in the transformation which yields the hypothetical sentence, from something that expresses an assertion to something that does not (whereas, on the performers' view, categorical commendations do get transformed into something else when they get inserted into conditional clauses). This, as before, misses the point. For, first of all, the critic, like all of us, has to explain how, having mastered the meaning of the speech act performed by the utterer of 'The cat is on the mat', we can go on to understand the speech act performed by the utterer of 'If the cat is on the mat it is purring'. For although the two speech acts are assertions, they are different assertions. And, secondly, the problem was about the word 'is' in 'The cat is on the mat' and about *its* indicative mood. This was explained in the categorical by reference to the speech act of assertion; but this 'is' is not, in the conditional, used to perform any assertion. The other 'is', in the second half of the sentence (the main verb) has, no doubt, the function of making the whole hypothetical sentence express an assertion; but what has become of the explanation of the meaning of the first 'is' (the one after 'cat') ? Unless its meaning can be explained indirectly in the way that I have been suggesting, what *does* it mean?

We have, therefore, shown that it is possible to take a sentence whose meaning has been explained partly by reference to a speech act, and transfer it into a conditional clause in which that speech act is not performed, without altering its meaning in any sense that would be damaging to *modus ponens*. Indeed, it is by understanding *modus ponens* that we understand the function of conditional clauses. It must be admitted, however, that this kind of explanation cannot be reproduced in the case of 'I promise'. For explicit performative verbs, for a reason which will shortly be explained, cannot be put into conditional clauses at all, as critics have noted. If, therefore, any performer were injudicious enough to claim that 'That is a good movie' meant the same as 'I commend that as a movie', he would be open to the objection that the definiendum can, but the definiens cannot, appear in conditional clauses. But he can escape this objection, as in the negative case, by being careful to put his thesis always in the form that sentences containing 'good' are commendations, and never in the form that they are equivalent to sentences beginning 'I commend'.

Is there, in fact, anything to prevent us treating 'That is a good movie', when it goes into a conditional clause, in exactly the same way as we have treated 'The cat is on the mat'? As before, we know the meaning of the hypothetical sentence form. And we know the meanings of the categoricals that are encaged in it. So we can easily perform the standard manœuvre for letting the consequent of the hypothetical out of its cage. Thus, if I am prepared to say that it is a good movie, and that if it is a good movie it will make a lot of money, I can go on to say 'It will make a lot of money'. The only difference between this and the preceding case is that to affirm the minor premiss 'It is a good movie' is here to commend the movie. But this does not make the meaning of 'It is a good movie' in the categorical premiss different from that of the same words in the conditional clause of the hypothetical premiss in any sense that is damaging to the inference, any more than the fact that 'The cat is on the mat' (categorical) is used to assert that the cat is on the mat, whereas the same words occurring in a conditional clause are not used to make this assertion, invalidated the inference we discussed earlier.

4. *Neustics, Tropics and Phrastics*

The limited argument of this paper is now complete. It was designed to show, first, that the appearance of a word in interrogatives, negatives, and conditional clauses provides no general argument against explaining its meaning in terms of the speech act standardly performed in categorical affirmative utterances containing it; and secondly that, once we understand the transformations which turn simple sentences into these more complex forms, we understand also how the words in them have meaning, even though the speech acts in terms of which their meaning was explained are no longer being performed. But it must be admitted that this whole region of meaning theory is still very obscure, and will not become clearer until much more work has been done on it. I will end, therefore, by just mentioning a technical device, invented by Frege and Russell, which can shed a little more light on the questions discussed above, and possibly explain the reasons for some of the phenomena noticed.

Russell, in *Principles of Mathematics* (§38), says that 'the p and the q which enter into [the proposition 'p implies q'] are not strictly the same as the p or the q which are separate propositions'. And he took over Frege's assertion sign in order to show how they were not the same. When a sentence occurs categorically and is used to make an assertion, it has the assertion sign in front of it; when it occurs in the conditional clause of an asserted hypothetical sentence, *it* has no assertion sign; the only assertion sign is that governing the whole hypothetical sentence.

There is, however, an important distinction to be made here which Russell did not make, and which, although I made it in some earlier unpublished work (pp. 22-4 above), I omitted to make when I took over the Frege-Russell device in *The Language of Morals* (chap. 2). In that book, I used a particle called the *neustic*, which did two jobs, one of them that of the Frege-Russell assertion sign (which itself has two functions, corresponding to the two strokes of Frege's sign; but we need not complicate the present issue by bringing in that distinction); the other job that my neustic did was that of a sign of mood to differentiate imperatives and indicatives. I now think that, in the supposed interests of simplicity, I sinned against the light by blurring the distinction between sign of mood and sign of subscription. The commonly used expression 'assertion sign' can easily lead us to ignore this distinction, and also that between assertion (whose content can be negative) and affirmation. For this sin I will now try to atone by using the term 'neustic' more narrowly for the sign of subscription to an assertion or other speech act, and inventing a new term '*tropic*' (from the Greek word for 'mood') for the sign of mood.

I shall retain the term '*phrastic*' for the part of sentences which is governed by the tropic and is common to sentences with different tropics. In internally negated sentences, it is perhaps best to treat the sign of negation as part of the phrastic; and it is possible that some other logical connectives should be so treated, but others should not. For example, the sign of external negation belongs outside the phrastic. It would be rash to broach this difficult subject here; I wish merely to emphasise, to avoid confusion, that the sign of internal negation is not, in my view, a tropic. The reader must not, therefore, confuse the narrower notion of 'tropic' with the wider notion of 'sentence form' used above.

When we say that 'The cat is on the mat' is a typical indicative (when we mention its mood, that is), we identify the type of speech act which it is standardly used to perform. Thus mood signs or tropics classify sentences according to the speech acts to which they are assigned by the conventions which give meanings to those signs. When we take a categorical sentence, however, and transfer it into a conditional clause, what happens? As it occurs categorically, the sentence has (1) a sign of mood or tropic; but also (2) a sign of subscription or neustic (expressed or understood). When it goes into the cage, it takes its tropic with it, but loses its neustic. The whole sentence in which it is encaged has a neustic, but not the conditional clause by itself. That, indeed, is what we mean when we say that when a hypothetical sentence of the form 'If p then q' is uttered, the statement corresponding to 'p' is not being asserted. But if the sentence were set out with its mood signs or tropics, 'p' would still have one.

What happens in 'if'-clauses also happens in many 'that'-clauses. In 'It is the case that p' and 'It is true that p' (two of the most vexed examples), the sentence substituted for 'p' will have a tropic and a phrastic but no neustic. It would be out of place to discuss here the difficult question of why 'It is the case that p' means (roughly) the same as 'p', and why 'It is not the case that p' means (roughly) the same as 'not p'. But it would be hasty and probably wrong to interpret 'It is not the case that' as either a tropic or a neustic or a combination of them. The whole sentence is complex, and its complexities need unravelling before we can give an account of any of its parts.

Although a sentence may have an indicative tropic, it cannot be used to make an assertion unless a neustic be added or understood. Neustics are normally understood with uttered sentences unless something special is done to indicate that they are not being subscribed to (for example, it is a convention that sentences written on the blackboard during philosophical, but not during historical, lectures are not being subscribed to). Forms of words like 'I hereby declare that' and 'I hereby order you to' are combinations of neustics and tropics. Professor J. R. Ross[1] has produced a number of arguments of a purely linguistic character which tend to show that an initial perform-

[1] 'On Declarative Sentences', in *Readings in Transformational Grammar*, ed. R. Jacobs and P. Rosenbaum.

ative expression of the general form 'I say to you that' occurs in the deep structure of all indicative sentences. If these arguments are cogent, they add force to much that I have said in this paper. They may also make us wonder quite how fundamental a feature of grammar it is that forbids explicit performatives in conditional clauses – a feature on which critics lay stress and which I have acknowledged. For if all categorical indicatives have an initial explicit performative in their deep structure, the fact that an explicit performative cannot go into a conditional clause cannot be used to differentiate indicatives from other moods or forms of sentences in any fundamental way. But since I am not competent to evaluate Ross's arguments, I shall not rely on them.

Now although a neustic has to be present or understood before a sentence can be used to make an assertion or perform any other speech act, it is in virtue of its tropic that it is used to make an assertion and not to perform some other speech act. And it carries this tropic with it into the cage of a conditional clause, leaving its neustic behind. This is why, when we want to uncage the consequent of a hypothetical by performing *modus ponens*, we have to use, as minor premiss, a proposition having the same tropic as the conditional clause. For example, the following is an *invalid* inference: 'If you are going to open the door, I am going to go; open the door; therefore I am going to go'. To make this into a valid inference, the second premiss, 'Open the door', has to be changed to 'You are going to open the door', which has the same indicative tropic as the conditional clause of the hypothetical.

The distinction between tropics and neustics helps to explain in what sense sentences change their meaning when they are put into conditional clauses, and in what sense they do not, and thus to interpret the two theses which I attributed to Searle in such a way that they do not conflict with one another. We can see this if we take the two hypothetical sentences we have been considering, 'If the cat is on the mat it is purring' and 'If it is a good movie it will make a lot of money', and ask how it can be that the following three statements, which are apparently inconsistent with one another, can nevertheless all be true:

(1) 'Good' and 'is' have the same meanings in the conditional clauses as they have in the corresponding categoricals.

(2) An explanation of their meanings in the corresponding categoricals has to include the fact that these are standardly used to perform the speech acts of commending and asserting respectively.

(3) In the conditional clauses, these speech acts are not performed.

These apparently mutually contradictory statements are all true, and are not really contradictory, because to be used to perform the speech acts, the clause in which the words appear would have to have a neustic, and this is lacking in the conditional clause. So, though the clause would turn into a commendation sentence or an assertion sentence if the word 'if' were removed and a neustic understood instead (it is *potentially* commendatory or assertoric, to use an old-fashioned term), it is not actually being used to perform the speech act specified by its tropic, because nobody is subscribing, by a neustic, to the speech act.

It would be a gross oversimplification to say that the word 'good' is itself a tropic or mood sign. When a performer says that it is a word used for commending, he does not mean this; rather he means that, in its analysis, which is undoubtedly complex, other tropics besides that of assertion will appear. What these are, and in what combination with the assertoric or indicative tropic, is a difficult question which I am not raising here. I am making only the defensive point that the fact that other tropics may figure in the analysis of this complex word besides the indicative tropic, and that therefore sentences containing it cannot be described without qualification as assertions, but have to be explained in terms of the more complex speech act of commending, is no bar to the appearance of the word in contexts where commending is not taking place, provided that the relation of these contexts to those in which it is taking place can be explained.[1]

---

[1] The reader is also referred to the following: Sir David Ross, *Foundations of Ethics* (Oxford, 1939) p. 33; P. T. Geach, 'Ascriptivism', *Philosophical Review*, LXIX (1960) 221, and 'Assertion', *Philosophical Review*, LXXIV (1965) 449; J. R. Searle, 'Meaning and Speech Acts', *Philosophical Review*, LXXI (1962), reprinted in Rollins (ed.), *Knowledge and Experience*, with discussion by others; P. Ziff, *Semantic Analysis*, p. 227; G. J. Warnock, in G. Pitcher (ed.), *Truth*, pp. 57 f., and *Contemporary Moral Philosophy*, p. 78; J. O. Urmson, *The Emotive Theory of Ethics*, chap. 11; H. N. Castañeda, in Castañeda and Nakhnikian (eds.), *Morality and the Language of Conduct*.

Appendix
REPLY TO MR G. J. WARNOCK

Mr Warnock has been kind enough to show me the typescript of a note on the above article which is to appear in the *Philosophical Review*.[1] We have also exchanged further notes privately. Although I have not (owing to timing problems) seen the version of his note which is actually to be printed, I think it may be useful to halt the press for long enough to comment on, and attempt to clarify, the issue between us.

The term 'speech act' itself has caused difficulties. Is it equivalent to 'illocutionary act', or is it more inclusive or more generic? And what is the criterion of identity for speech acts – do 'Go East' and 'Go West' express the same speech act, because they are both pieces of advice, or different ones, because the advice is different? On the first question, prompted by Warnock's mention of Austin's use, I looked through *How to do Things with Words*, and found only four occurrences (though I may have missed some). On pp. 52 and 147 the expression 'total speech act' seems to mean *all* that is done in saying something, including the phonetic, phatic and rhetic acts, the locutionary and illocutionary and perhaps even the perlocutionary acts. On p. 149 'speech act' is used twice, once in the phrase 'the theory of speech acts', which does little to determine its precise meaning, and once to refer to illocutionary acts in particular, which Austin is about to attempt to classify. I do not, however, suggest that even here 'speech act' *means* 'illocutionary act'. My own use is much the same as Austin's; I might call all these different kinds of acts 'speech acts' in a wide sense; but since I am talking almost exclusively about illocutionary acts, not much difference would be made if, wherever I have used the expression 'speech act', the more cumbrous but also more precise term 'illocutionary act' were substituted.

However, I have argued in the paper which follows that the

[1] LXXX (1971).

distinction between locutionary and illocutionary acts is in any case impossible to sustain; and so for me the criteria of identity for both must be the same. Austin might in theory have used different criteria, saying that 'Go East' and 'Go West' expressed different locutionary acts but the same illocutionary act. But I know of no evidence that he would have said this. Indeed, to say this would be quite at variance with our normal use of the word 'act' (that two acts are of the same kind does not make them the same act). For my own part, I would say that 'Go East' and 'Go West' express different illocutionary acts, though illocutionary acts of the same kind. In saying one of them one is giving different advice, and thus doing a different thing, from what one is giving and doing in saying the other. I have found no evidence that Austin used the expressions differently from this, though it is possible that he sometimes says 'act' when he means 'kind of act', and possible even that I have done this myself, in contexts which make it clear that this is what we are doing. There are, however, more problems about the criteria for identity of speech acts than can even be raised here.

Secondly, Warnock asks whether my thesis is one about *certain* words only (e.g. 'good'), or about *all* words: i.e. am I saying that all words (and all sentences) have to have their meaning explained, at least partly, by giving the illocutionary acts to whose performance they contribute, or am I only saying that this is true of certain words? The answer is that I think the thesis defensible for all words, but that in the above article I am seeking to defend it only for certain words, and only against one particular argument which has been widely canvassed.

Thirdly, Warnock says that Professor Searle is not, as I think, my ally, because he is talking about *sentences* when he issues the manifesto which I quote approvingly at the beginning of my article, whereas my thesis is one about *words*. I cannot see that this makes any difference. Sentences mean what they mean because of what the words in them mean; and, conversely, to know what a word means is to know what difference is made to the meaning of sentences in which it occurs by the fact that that word is used and not others. My view about 'good' and Searle's about 'promise' could be put either in terms of words or in terms of sentences; and I at any rate was extremely careful, when I stated the 'performers'' claim on the second page of my article, to tie words, sentences and speech acts together in a way in which any complete account of the meaning of any of them must tie them together.

Searle himself, I fear, will not be willing to be enrolled as my ally, because my article has the form of a rebuttal of his earlier criticisms, for which, to judge by their reappearance in his recent book, he still has a parental affection. It does seem, however, as if his latest pronouncements, with which, unlike Warnock, I am in almost complete agreement, are inconsistent, at least in spirit, with his earlier attack on the 'performers'. Perhaps he will come to see this, or else explain why it is not so. Still, ally or not, I should like to defend Searle against what I think is a misunderstanding by Warnock of his argument on pp. 18–21 of *Speech Acts*. When Searle says (p. 18) that 'every possible speech act *can in principle* be given an exact formulation', this fairly weak claim is strong enough to serve his argument; he does not need (and does not therefore put forward) the stronger claim that the speech acts performed in the utterance of sentences *are* all, always, exactly formulated. Warnock therefore misses Searle's point when he objects that this stronger thesis is false (as it is). Searle's argument (if I may be so bold as to summarise it) was that, since one can always in principle formulate one's speech act explicitly in words so that the meaning of the sentence used (including its reference – see below) determines the speech act exactly, it is always open to us to study the speech act by formulating it explicitly and studying the meaning of the resulting sentence; and that, correspondingly, the meaning of any fully explicit sentence can be studied by studying the nature of the complete speech act which it can be used to perform. Thus the two studies collapse into one another.

We must not, of course, confuse sentence-meaning with utterer's meaning; but they are closely related. The meaning of a fully explicit sentence (one in which the speaker has said in full what he means) determines what he must mean if he is using the words in it correctly (as he must be, if he has said what he means), and determines, similarly, to what he must be referring if he is following the 'demonstrative conventions' (Austin's term from *Philosophical Papers*, p. 90) correctly. If he says 'my left hand', he must be referring to his left hand, or he is misusing the words. It thus determines what speech act he is performing. What Warnock calls 'the circumstances of the utterance and the intentions of the speaker' are therefore not, as he seems to think, 'something additional' to what is thus determined by the meanings of the words, so that enquiry into this 'something additional' makes the study of speech acts into something more than the study of meanings. For the meaning, if (as Searle proposes) it is made explicit, will determine what the intentions and the circumstances have to be, if the speech act is to be validly and sincerely performed. And when Warnock says 'we *do* have to assume an appropriate context of utterance – that is, not *just* know what the sentences mean', he entirely neglects the possibility that we cannot be said to know what they mean unless we know what would be (linguistically) appropriate contexts of utterance. To say this, however, is not to assent to all the extravagant things that have been said about the relation of context and intention to meaning, many of which rest on a confusion of illocutionary with perlocutionary acts.

Warnock next offers what he says is a good reason for a conclusion for which he calls my own reason a bad one: viz. the conclusion that the meaning of 'promise' is to be explained in terms of the speech act of promising. His reason is that 'promise' is actually 'the *word for* the speech act'. I agree that this is a good reason, though ambiguously stated. By 'the word for' Warnock here seems to mean 'the word used to describe' and not 'the word used to perform'. In criticism of my own reason, he points out (correctly) that it is only a contingent fact about language that the words used to describe speech acts are often the same as the words used to perform them. But that this is no criticism of my own reason (which is, that 'promise' is the word used to perform the speech act of promising, and that this is part of its meaning) is evident if we make the experiment of supposing that this contingent fact was not a fact – i.e. that we had different words for performing and for describing the speech act of promising (as we have for marrying, which cannot be done by saying 'I marry you'). Let us suppose that we used the word 'promise' for performing, but the word 'undertake' for describing, the act, and that the words were not interchangeable. In that case the word 'promise' could still not have its meaning explained without saying that it was the word used for *performing* the act. And it follows from this that, since, in current usage as distinct from our imagined usage, it has this use among others, its meaning in *this* use cannot be explained without saying that it has this use; and it therefore follows that no account of the current meaning of the word is complete which omits to mention this fact.

It seems also to be Warnock's view that I am right in what I say about mood-signs (which, be it noted, are used to perform, not describe, speech acts of asserting, etc.). In his own words, 'If it is the primary, essential function of a certain word to signal that, in the utterance of a sentence in which it occurs, a certain speech act is standardly performed, then all too obviously the meaning of *that* word will have to be explained, at least in part, in terms of that speech act'. It bothers me not at all that this is 'all too obviously true' or a 'truism'. The burden of my argument was that, when the matter is fully understood (and I hope that my article and this note will have contributed to such an understanding), the 'critic' cannot assent to this truism, and to the equally obviously true statement that all sentences have to contain, explicitly or implicitly, such a 'signal', without being compelled to such absurdities as denying the validity of all *modus ponens* arguments. For example, if an explanation of the meaning of 'He has gone East' has to say that its utterer performs, standardly, the illocutionary act of stating that the person referred to has gone East, then in the conditional clause 'if he has gone East' the meaning of 'he has gone East' would be, by the 'critics'' argument, different in meaning, since this act is not being performed; so this *modus ponens* is invalidated by equivocation. And the same would be true *whatever* the categorical premiss was and *whatever* speech act entered into the explanation of its meaning.

In any case, even if the general thesis that an explanation of the meanings of *some* words has to bring in speech acts is truistic, this is not the case with the thesis that the explanation of a particular word ('good') has to bring in a particular kind of speech act (commending). The latter thesis is, however, defended in my other writings and not in this article, which only tries to remove one objection to it. Warnock as good as admits that it is successful in this; but he complains that, although I 'would claim only to have removed certain objections' to my doctrine, I have not offered any reason for supposing it to be actually correct. But neither has Warnock, in his note, offered any reason for supposing it to be *in*correct. He contents himself with saying that 'good' is 'obviously *not* the *sort* of word for which there has emerged any reason to suppose that speech acts must come into explanations of meanings'. So what Warnock says is the 'central objection' to my view is a bare assertion on his part that there is nothing to be said for it.

6 Austin's Distinction between Locutionary and Illocutionary Acts

Towards the end of *How to do Things with Words*,[1] in what may be regarded as the final version of his doctrine (so far as anything in the book can be called final), Austin makes a threefold distinction between locutionary, illocutionary and perlocutionary acts. I shall not in this paper be saying much about the distinction between illocutionary and perlocutionary acts, which I have maintained elsewhere in other terms.[2] I think it of great importance – which is not to say that it is entirely plain sailing; the neglect of this distinction has perhaps done more in recent years to confuse people, especially in ethics, than any other single mistake. However, I shall mention this distinction only in passing, and shall concentrate on the other, between locutionary and illocutionary acts – a distinction to which Austin attached equal importance, but which to me is so unclear that I am tempted to say that it cannot be sustained.

It will perhaps be clearest if I begin with a summary historical account of how Austin arrived at this distinction. The distinction was arrived at in the course of an attempt to sort out the difficulties attending the earlier distinction between performative and constative utterances; and we must therefore first see what was wrong with that earlier distinction. I remember that in 1958, at the conference at Royaumont, Austin read a paper called 'Performatif–Constatif';[3] this was in fact a statement of

   This paper was read, in an earlier form, to a class given by Mr J. O. Urmson and myself at Oxford in 1963. I am most grateful to him for his help, especially on historical points.
   [1] Pp. 94 ff. References are to this work unless otherwise stated.
   [2] 'Freedom of the Will', *Ar. Soc. Supp.*, xxv (1950); reprinted in *Essays on the Moral Concepts* (forthcoming).
   [3] *La Philosophie analytique*, Cahiers de Royaumont (Paris, 1962) p. 271 (hereafter referred to as *PC*).

Hitherto unpublished.

the performative–constative doctrine which is to be found in the early part of *How to do Things with Words*; that this doctrine raises difficulties is mentioned (the difficulties, of course, which are raised against it in *How to do Things with Words*). This book had been delivered as the William James Lectures at Harvard three years previously, and was in substance written a good deal earlier, since Austin lectured on 'Words and Deeds' in Oxford from 1952 to 1954, and, to judge by my pupils' reports of the lectures, and by what Mr Urmson, his editor, has told me, the substance of them was much the same as we have in the book. In particular, the locutionary–illocutionary distinction was already there.

I think it highly significant that in preparing a paper to be delivered to the French, whom he assumed to be beginners in this sort of philosophy, Austin decided to give them just the original performative–constative distinction, and to leave the later doctrine out of the picture. This shows that at that time he thought it necessary to grasp the earlier doctrine as an introduction to the later; this was a rather strange procedure, because by that time he had seen quite clearly that the earlier doctrine would not do. The same attitude to the earlier doctrine is evident in the arrangement of *How to do Things with Words*; we are taken (albeit with caveats) steadily through the earlier doctrine; then it is shown to create difficulties; then the later doctrine is introduced as a way of salvaging what is of value in the earlier. I do not think that Austin would have adopted this method of exposition if he had not retained a great affection for the old distinction (which had, after all, come to be regarded as his greatest discovery – as in a manner of speaking it was – and was already being used, and misused, all over the place by other philosophers).

The philosophical importance of all this is that considerable traces of the old distinction survive in the new distinction between locution and illocution; and I am going to be so bold as to claim that these vestigial traces to a great extent confuse the issue that he is trying to clarify. If, therefore, we find difficulties, as I do, in the locutionary–illocutionary distinction, we may be able to attribute them to the malign influence of the old distinction. (For the close connexion between the two distinctions, see Austin, p. 144.)

What then is wrong with the old performative–constative

distinction? I think that what is wrong with it can be put most clearly in the following way: it is not the way Austin uses, but he seemed to accept it when I put it to him at the Royaumont conference (*PC*, p. 283). There is not just one distinction, but two; and these two distinctions got inextricably muddled up through the use of the word 'performative' to mark both of them – not so much by Austin as by other philosophers. Nevertheless, they were to be pardoned, since nowhere in the works published in his lifetime did he make the matter clear. There is first the distinction between different things that we can be doing in saying something (what he later called the different illocutionary forces that an utterance can have). Examples are: making a statement; giving an order; asking a question. And secondly, there is the distinction between the two different ways of doing the *same* thing which Austin called 'primary' and 'explicit' performatives. The following table sets out these two different distinctions in terms of examples.

	(a) *Primary*	(b) *Explicit*
(1) *Promising*	I shall be there.[1]	I promise that I shall be there.[1]
(2) *Ordering*	Shut the door.	I order you to shut the door.
(3) *Questioning*	Is he honest?	I ask you whether he is honest.
(4) *Stating*	He's not at home.	I tell you he's not at home.

The reason why it is easy to confuse these two distinctions is that in some of the obvious examples they are both in evidence. Austin seems to have started by contrasting pairs of utterances like 'I promise that I shall be there' and 'He's not at home', (1b) and (4a). (There is a historical reason for this: as Austin makes clear in several places,[2] the germ of his whole approach to this subject lay in his reflection upon two things that were in the forefront of discussion in 1939, when he first formed, as he says, 'the views which underlie these lectures'. These were the controversies surrounding the verification theory of meaning

---

[1] Austin's example (p. 69). In my dialect, 'will' would be more normal than 'shall' in both cases.

[2] e.g. pp. 2 f.; *Philosophical Papers*, pp. 220 f.

and its near-relative the emotive theory of ethics. Austin thought – along with others – that the way out of these controversies was to recognise (1) that the so-called factual proposition which was singled out as alone meaningful by the verification-criterion of meaningfulness was in fact only *one kind* of meaningful utterance; (2) that the many other kinds of utterances that there are were not to be lumped together, but carefully distinguished; and (3) that they were not to be accorded a logically inferior status, as hardly worth the notice of serious logicians. The fact that this was the origin of Austin's views explains a great deal about their development; it explains, for example, how he came to his important doctrine about infelicities; I am sure that, though in fact the main importance of the doctrine is something quite different, what led him to it was a desire to show that, though 'performatives' cannot be true or false, they are subject to other analogous disciplines which ought to make even verificationists stop looking down their noses at them.)

But to return; if we consider the two utterances 'He's not at home' and 'I promise that I shall be there', we see that the first one is a fine specimen of the verifiable empirical statement, and the second is not. And there is also another difference between them, namely that whereas the first (4a) is, in Austin's terminology, a *primary* utterance, the second (1b) is an *explicit* performative. That this is a different point from the distinction between statements and promises can be brought out quite easily. If the promise had been expressed in a primary way, by saying 'I shall be there', then both it and (4a) would have been primary utterances; if, on the other hand, the statement 'He's not at home' (4a) had been expressed in an explicit way, by saying 'I tell you that he's not at home', then both it and (1b) would have been explicit performatives (in one sense of the ambiguous word 'performatives'); but in neither of these two cases would the other distinction, that between the different kinds of speech-act called stating and promising, have been abolished. So these two distinctions (that between different kinds of speech-act, and that between different ways of performing the same kind of speech-act) are in fact quite independent. But I do not think that Austin at first realised this; and I am fairly certain that nobody else realised it at first, though I remember realising it myself fairly early on. This would account for the strange reluctance Austin from time to time evinces to saying that utterances like 'I state that the cat is on the mat' could be called performatives. (Urmson has expressed to me the opinion that the reluctance was only being put on, as a piece of showmanship; I think that perhaps when he originally wrote these passages (which occur already in the earliest drafts) they expressed a sincere reluctance, but that he retained them in later versions as (partly) showmanship.) He speaks as if to admit 'I state' as a performative would be to make nonsense of the whole distinction, and render all his work nugatory. Notice, for example, p. 65, where he mentions, as one objection to the use of the first-person/other-persons asymmetry as a way of distinguishing performative utterances from the rest, the fact that in that case 'We shall be in apparent danger of bringing in many formulas which we might not like to class as performatives; for example "I state that" (to utter which *is* to state) as well as "I bet that"'. And on p. 68 he says '"I state that" seems to conform to our grammatical or quasi-grammatical requirements: but do we want *it* in? Our criterion, such as it is, seems in danger of letting in non-performatives.' I do not think that Austin would have felt a difficulty here if, when he wrote this, he had been clear about there being two distinctions and not just one. For, if it were the explicit–primary distinction that was in question, there would be no objection to admitting 'I state that' on the same side of it as 'I bet that' or 'I promise that'; and this is the distinction that the 'grammatical' criterion that he is talking about usually serves to mark; on the other hand, if it were the other distinction, that between different kinds of speech-act, that he was looking for a way of making, it would be only too obvious that the kind of grammatical difference that he is talking about here (namely the first-person/other-persons asymmetry) could never serve to make this.

The root of the trouble is that the original distinction ought never to have been put in terms of *saying* something versus *doing* something. For there is no relevant sense of 'doing something' in which *all* cases of saying something are not doing something; for to say anything (in the sense of 'say' which here concerns us) is to perform some kind of speech-*act*. It ought rather to have been put in terms of *doing* different kinds of thing, one of which (only) is stating. Once we have seen this, the word 'performative' comes to appear a bad one, and indeed a thoroughly misleading one; for it is not particularly apposite for marking the explicit–primary distinction; and, if it is used to mark the distinction between different kinds of speech-act, it suggests two falsehoods: one is that stating is not doing anything; the other is that all other things that we do in speech-acts, apart from stating, share some common feature, which distinguishes them all from stating. But it is not in the least clear what this feature could be. And indeed, once, bearing in mind these distinctions, we ask how we tell which utterances go into the constative class, we are in great difficulties. If stating does, does declaring or affirming? Then does swearing or betting? If we looked at the matter without prejudice, I think we should, as perhaps Austin later did, class all these acts together for certain purposes. Obviously what is needed is not a dichotomy between constative utterances and the rest, but a complete classification of all kinds of speech-act; and it was this that Austin in the end saw to be necessary.

So, then, the performative–constative distinction, immensely fruitful and important as it was, had to be abandoned. But, on its way out, it engendered the locutionary–illocutionary distinction; and I think that this itself is open to grave objection, and that it might never have been produced in the form in which we have it but for the historical reason that Austin was trying to salvage something of his original distinction.

My difficulty with the later distinction will be clear if we ask what a locutionary act, as distinct from an illocutionary act, is supposed to be. It is defined as including 'the utterance of certain noises, the utterance of certain words in a certain construction, and the utterance of them with a certain "meaning" in the favourite philosophical sense of that word, i.e. with a certain sense and with a certain reference' (p. 94). It would appear that, since the locutionary act already contains the use of words with a sense and reference, what distinguishes the illocutionary act – the illocutionary force – must be something different from the sense and reference of the words.

Let us for a moment dwell on this word 'sense', and notice another historical point. The pair of terms 'sense and reference' recalls Frege, though I will not attempt to enquire what the relation was between Frege's *Sinn und Bedeutung* and other earlier pairs such as *intension* and *extension*, or *connotation* and *denotation*. What we must notice is that all these are possessed typically or primarily by words or terms, not by sentences or propositions.

For example, 'the morning star' and 'the evening star' were said to have different senses but the same reference. Austin, also, speaks of 'the utterance of *words* with a certain sense and with a certain reference'. In saying this, I do not wish to deny that philosophers did sometimes speak of the sense of sentences or of propositions (the important distinction between sentences and propositions need not here detain us). I wish to say only that when we hear the word 'sense' used in this semi-technical sense, it is the sense of a word or of a phrase that we naturally think of rather than the sense of a whole sentence.

Nor do we naturally think of all words as equally possessing sense. Here the history of the notion can again help us. From Socrates and Plato onwards sense, and its ancestor intension (like extension, the ancestor of Frege's *Bedeutung*), have been most commonly thought of as attaching to the sorts of terms for which we use nouns and adjectives and other predicates and subjects. It has been applied only by courtesy, as it were, to parts of sentences which do not fall into this class. (Hence, by the way, the stubborn attempts to treat 'exists' as a predicate, and so give it a respectable sense.) We do not so naturally (or at any rate many people did not so naturally) think of 'if' as having a sense (Plato never, so far as I know, felt the need of a Platonic Idea of ifness). The verb 'is' was treated as having sense, but only because it was thought to be or connote a predicate.

The origin of this exclusiveness is what Professor Ryle calls the 'Fido'–Fido theory of meaning;[1] it is natural to suppose that what have meaning in the proper sense are nouns and adjectives, because *some* plausibility can be given to the doctrine that nouns and adjectives *stand for* things which are their meanings, as 'Fido' is thought to stand for the dog Fido who is *its* meaning. But not much plausibility can be given to a similar treatment of 'if', or for that matter of 'is'. I should hesitate to say that we have yet got philosophy clear of the notion that meaning is something which attaches primarily to subject-words and predicate-words – a notion which has sometimes led to an unjust neglect of other parts of speech.

If to perform a locutionary act is to utter words with a certain sense and reference, but not, *qua* locutionary act, with any

[1] See 'The Theory of Meaning', in *British Philosophy in the Mid-Century*, ed. C. A. Mace.

illocutionary force, what is going to count as a locutionary act? Suppose I say 'The cat is on the mat'. Here the expression 'the cat' and 'the mat' have, presumably, a sense and a reference. What about the word 'on'? That, we may allow, has a sense but no reference. But what about the word 'is'? Here we seem to be faced with a dilemma. It certainly has no reference, except, of course, the temporal reference to the present time. Has it a sense? Well, of course it has a meaning; but has it a sense in the narrow interpretation of that word as, apparently, used by Austin, which excludes illocutionary force? I should be inclined to say that the meaning of the word 'is' is complex. There is, first of all, the notion which I shall call 'predication' – the notion of something *being* something. But then there is also the notion of *stating* or *asserting that* something is something (as opposed to asking whether it is, or commanding that it be, or promising that it will be). This is the *tropic* element in its meaning (see p. 89 above). The notion which I call predication is common to, for example, statements and commands; I can either state that the cat will be on the mat or command that the cat be on the mat. Predication belongs in the *phrastics* of sentences. But the notion of assertion belongs to the *tropic*; it is confined to statements and the like. Yet we cannot say anything without including in what we say some tropic or sign of mood; in other words, if we *say* anything, it has to be a statement or a command or a question or a promise or something else belonging to this classification; it has, in fact, to be some kind of speech-act, and therefore have some kind of illocutionary force. Stating something is not merely predicating; it is also asserting, and the expression of the statement has to include an indication that it is asserting, and not, for example, asking or commanding.

So, then, the dilemma that we are faced with is this. Let it be granted that the word 'is' in the statement 'The cat is on the mat' has, as part of its sense, the notion of predication; so let us forget about that. But it also has, as part of its sense, the notion of assertion – what tells us that this is a statement and not a command or a question. The dilemma is this: Is this part of the sense, as Austin was using that word? If it is, then Austin will have to admit – as I suspect that in fact he would have admitted – that the sense, at least sometimes, and indeed so far as I can see, always, includes part, at any rate, of the illocutionary force. For if the fact that it is a statement that is being made and not a command given forms part of its sense, then this is to specify, already, what kind of illocutionary act it is (for commands and statements are kinds of illocutionary acts). So on this horn of the dilemma the distinction between locutionary and illocutionary acts breaks down; for we have shown that, even if the locutionary act consists in no more than uttering words with a certain sense and reference, this would have to include, in the *sense* (on this horn of the dilemma), a specification of whether it is a statement or a command, etc.; but these are illocutionary acts. So, on this horn of the dilemma, one cannot perform a locutionary act completely without specifying (at any rate partly) the illocutionary force which the act carries.

I am fairly sure that this is the horn of the dilemma that Austin would have chosen (although I know that Urmson disagrees with me about this). Austin says, on p. 145, 'neither of these abstractions is so very expedient' (the abstractions being those performed when we attend, as in the 'performative utterance' on his view, to the illocutionary force, and neglect 'the dimension of correspondence with facts', or when, on the contrary, we attend to the locutionary aspects of the speech-act and abstract from the illocutionary). The use of the (pejorative?) word 'abstraction' here seems to me to indicate that Austin, if pressed, might have in the end admitted that the distinction between locutionary and illocutionary cannot be sustained; or at any rate that locution essentially brings with it illocutionary force. It is not merely that all locutionary acts are also illocutionary acts; it is that being *that* locutionary act – which involves being a use of words with *that* sense – makes the act, already, into an act carrying a certain illocutionary force.

The other horn of the dilemma is much worse. It consists of saying that it is no part of the sense of any of the words uttered in a locutionary act to tell us whether it is, e.g., a question or a statement or a command or a promise. But this would mean that in performing a locutionary act we would not have made clear which of these things we were doing. But if, when a man had said something, he had not indicated whether he was stating a fact or telling me to do something or asking me a question, I should not be prepared to agree that he had finished saying what he intended to say; he would be in no better case than a man who left out any of the other essential bits of a sentence – a man who, for example, said 'has gone' without saying *who* had gone, or said 'John hit' but did not say whom he hit, or said 'Two (*cough, splutter*) two makes four', but did not say whether he meant 'two plus two makes four', or 'two times two makes four', or even 'two minus two makes four'. I doubt whether Austin or anyone else would call these complete locutionary acts; and in the same way to utter a sentence without showing whether it is in the indicative or the imperative mood (thus giving the utterance an illocutionary force) is to fail to complete the locutionary act.

A word should perhaps be said at this point about Austin's use (or more accurately, his studied avoidance) of the notion of *meaning*.[1] It is a notoriously vague notion, and I am sure that it would be quite wrong to think that Austin, in distinguishing as he does between the locutionary and the illocutionary act, is wanting to draw a hard-and-fast distinction, as some of his disciples seem to want to do, between meaning and illocutionary force. He says that the locutionary act involves the utterance of certain words 'with a certain "meaning" in the favourite philosophical sense of that word, i.e. with a certain sense and with a certain reference'. Elsewhere, he on the whole avoids the word, as if he felt that it was too vague a word to make precise what he wanted to say. Therefore, although he certainly *could* be interpreted as saying that meaning (in this favourite philosophical sense) is one thing, and illocutionary force another – and this, as we have seen, would be wrong, because 'sense', which he includes in meaning, itself includes illocutionary force – he could alternatively be interpreted as saying that the 'favourite philosophical sense' of 'meaning' is too narrow a concept to say what needs to be said about the use of words and sentences. Perhaps he might have agreed that in a wider sense of 'meaning' the illocutionary force *is* part of the meaning of an utterance. But probably, just because of the vacillation of the word 'meaning' between these wider and narrower senses, and because of the ingrained habit of *philosophers* (a tribe whose ingrained habits he never tired of castigating) of confining the word to 'sense and reference', he preferred not to use the word. In any case, nothing much hangs on whether we use it or not. I may be right or wrong about the illocutionary–locutionary distinction; but I am sure that the really crucial distinction is between

[1] See Appendix, pp. 115 f. below.

meaning in the wide sense (characterising both locutionary and illocutionary acts because both are governed by rules or conventions) and perlocutionary effects or intended effects, which are not so governed. The word 'pragmatics', which excludes meaning in the narrow sense, but includes both illocutionary force and perlocutionary force in a heterogeneous jumble, has caused much confusion in this area.

In the rest of this paper I want to consider a possible modification or reinterpretation of the locutionary–illocutionary distinction which might be thought to get over the difficulties I have raised. It might be said that in the locutionary act *part* of the illocutionary force is always specified; but that distinctions between illocutionary forces go far beyond what needs to be specified in the locutionary act in order to make it a complete locutionary act. It might be said, further, that the locutionary act has elements of meaning which have nothing to do with the illocutionary force; the reference might be a claimant for this status, and it might be claimed that certain elements in the sense are independent of the illocutionary force. It might be claimed, for example, that since the word 'green' obviously means the same in indicatives and imperatives, its meaning must be independent of the illocutionary force of these utterances.

If both these contentions were true, we should have a much more complicated situation than could be dealt with by the simple locutionary–illocutionary distinction. We should have at least a threefold division of elements of meaning – in the wide sense:

(1) those which are essential to the locutionary act but are independent of the illocutionary;
(2) those which are essential to the locutionary act but also determine the illocutionary force;
(3) those which are concerned with the illocutionary act but are external to the locutionary.

These two contentions are independent of one another; so we must discuss them separately. Take first the claim that the distinction between illocutionary forces goes far beyond what needs to be specified in the locutionary act itself in order to make it complete. The following example might be cited: if someone says 'Shut the door', I am not, indeed, fully apprised of the sense of his utterance until I have gathered that it is in the imperative mood; but I do not have, in addition, to know whether it is an order, or a request, or a piece of advice; the distinction between these kinds of illocutionary force does not affect the sense of the utterance.

This contention is on the face of it true; but it is possible through confusion to draw false inferences from it. When the man has said 'Shut the door', he has told me to shut the door. *Telling to* is a generic illocutionary act which has as species *ordering to, requesting to, advising to, instructing to, praying to,* etc. If anyone disputes whether praying to is a species of telling to, let him consider the following example: a man prays for rain, but when God sends rain it ruins his wife's washing on the line; he is unreasonably angry with God; but when God sees this, he appears to the man and says 'But you did tell me to send you some rain'.

I wish to lay stress on this genus–species relationship, because it seems to me to be the key to the matter. Let us first observe the operation of a similar relationship in a case where differences of mood or differences between kinds of commands or kinds of statement are not in question. I say to my wife 'There's an animal in the back yard'. Now 'animal' has more generic and more specific senses; in the most generic sense, my proposition would be true if our daughter were in the back yard; and it would be true if there were at least one bacillus in the back yard. There are at least two interpretations of what I actually meant. One is that I meant the word generically; I was not intending to convey more than that there was, in the zoological sense, an animal there; for all I cared, it might be a bacterium or a hyena or Aunt Maud. Another possibility is that I meant the word more specifically; I should not have called my statement true if there were merely a bacillus or even an insect, or a human being, in the back yard; I *meant* (in one sense of that word) that there was a non-human mammal in the back yard.

Here it is necessary to guard against an easy mistake; otherwise people may either commit it or, if they are brighter, accuse me of committing it. I do not think that generality is the same thing as ambiguity; that is to say, I am not confusing what happens when I say 'animal' in the generic sense, and simply do not specify what kind of animal, with what happens when I say 'animal', but do not make it clear whether I am using that word in the generic or in a more specific sense. It is the latter case that we are concerned with.

Coming back now to illocutionary forces: suppose that I say 'Shut the door'; and suppose that I am a colonel, and the addressee, let us say, a captain. It might be unclear, in such a case, whether this was a request or an order. Worse, I might not myself have specified, even to myself, which it was; if the captain then shut the door, neither of us would need to enquire which it was. This is parallel to the case when I say to my wife 'There's an animal in the back yard', and she looks out and sees a panther, and in the ensuing commotion none of us asks, or needs to ask, whether I meant 'animal' in the generic or in a more specific sense. Or, to take a less alarming case, suppose that it was one of our neighbours' cats; do we ever have to enquire whether, if it had been one of our neighbours' children, I would have called it an animal? These troubles never trouble us when we are talking about subject and predicate expressions – logicians take it for granted that these sorts of ambiguity can arise, and, if need be, can be sorted out. But when it comes to illocutionary forces, which up till now have been unfamiliar ground, all sorts of things get said which would never be said in the other case, although the cases are very comparable.

When I say 'Shut the door', and do not specify whether it is an order, I may be simply giving the utterance the *generic* illocutionary force of an imperative, and just not caring or specifying whether it is an order or a request or a piece of advice. But suppose that the captain says, unexpectedly, 'I won't'. *Then* I shall have to decide: Do I intend it as an order or just a request? I shall have to say, either 'Oh, never mind if you don't want to', or 'I order you to shut it'. Similarly, if my wife were to say (equally surprisingly) 'Animal? What do you mean?', I might have to decide whether I meant it in the generic sense or in some more specific sense. I do not mean to imply that I must have been, all along, using it in the sense in which I finally decided to use it. Very likely I did not, originally, think in what sense I was using it; to that extent the later utterances 'I order you to shut the door' and 'There's a non-human mammal in the back yard' are not the equivalents of the original utterances; they are improvements on them – I have made them less equivocal.

The proposal before us is that we allow the fact that the

utterance 'Shut the door' was an imperative to count as part of the sense of the utterance, and therefore as partially determining what locutionary act it was; but that when the specification is given that it was an order, this should be said to be no part of the sense, but only part of the illocutionary force. This seems to be putting the dividing line in an awkward place – though there is no absolute bar to putting it there. It seems to me that it would be more convenient and less misleading to say

(1) in the case in which I had not thought whether or not it was an order that I was giving, that my original utterance had the generic illocutionary force of an imperative, and that this was part of its sense; and that my subsequent utterance 'I order you to shut the door' had the specific illocutionary force of an order, and that this also was part of its sense;

(2) in the case where I did originally intend it as an order, but had to go on to say 'I order you to shut the door' or 'That was an order', to make it clear to the captain what I meant, that all along my utterance had the specific illocutionary force, and therefore the sense, of an order, but that I did not make this clear until afterwards. This would be like having all along meant 'non-human mammal', but having failed to make it clear that this was what I meant until it became apparent that I was not being understood. *I* meant 'non-human mammal'; but my *words* could have meant something more generic.

I conclude that it is much more convenient to say that the illocutionary force, whether or not it is specified or made clear, is always part of the sense, and that therefore the distinction between locutionary and illocutionary breaks down even in its amended form.

Let us now consider the other claim, that there are parts of the sense of the locutionary act which have nothing to do with its illocutionary force. This might be interpreted as another way of saying something which I have myself in the past maintained; that is, that, e.g., statements and commands may have a common element, which I called the phrastic. Into this part of a sentence, which commands and statements (and promises and lots of other things) can share, will go everything except what I now call the tropic, which is the indicator of illocutionary force. I still think that this is true. But a phrastic is not a complete sentence; these elements of meaning never add up to a complete locutionary act – that, I think, the preceding discussion has made clear. For certain logical purposes, especially when, as most logicians do, we confine ourselves to one mood, the indicative, it is possible to operate just with phrastics and ignore tropics. This is the element of truth in the contention that there could be a constative utterance (the logicians' darling) which was not performative; but this constative utterance would *not* be a statement, but only, to use Austin's word, an abstraction from one; for in it the part which makes it a statement would have been omitted.

It is important to stress that, even with words like 'green', though they have in a way a meaning of their own, their meaning is an abstraction from the meanings of the sentences used in performing the speech-acts in which they occur or could occur, such as statements that something is green or is not green, commands to make something green, promises that it shall be made green, and so on. In support of this contention I offer the following fact: we could not *learn* the word 'green' except in the context of speech-acts containing it. Normally these speech-acts, whereby we learn a word like 'green', are statements; but they could be commands (cf. the beginning of the *Philosophical Investigations*). Having got to this point, however, it becomes tremendously important to stress the distinction, found in Austin but not – at any rate not at all conspicuously – in Wittgenstein, between illocutionary and perlocutionary acts. For, when I say that elements of meaning which are common to different kinds of speech-act are nevertheless abstractions from the total speech-acts in which the words having them occur, I do not want to be taken to be subscribing to the fashionable, very wide, extension of the concept of meaning to include all sorts of things that would more properly be included under Austin's perlocutionary effect – things which may be, for example, not a matter of any sort of convention but which have to be divined from the particular situation in which the utterance is made – the context, in one of the senses of that frightfully ambiguous word. I feel the need – but also the difficulty – of drawing the line (or *a* line); and I feel that a fuller discussion of Austin's notion might enable us to draw it with greater precision than I, at any rate, can so far.

Appendix

AUSTIN'S USE OF THE WORD 'MEANING' AND ITS COGNATES IN *HOW TO DO THINGS WITH WORDS*

Looking through the book, I have found occurrences of these words on pp. 7, 22, 33, 50, 94, 97, 98, 100, 108, 115 n., 120, 137, 138 and 148. Although some of these pages contain more than one occurrence, it does seem as if, for a work on such a topic, the words occur surprisingly rarely – or perhaps not surprisingly, if we realise that Austin had a distaste for them. Of these occurrences, those on pp. 7, 22 and 50 are casual uses (e.g. 'I mean, for example, the following', p. 22) which shed no light on our topic; and those on pp. 33, 108, 115 n. and 120 are mere anticipations or repetitions, in summary form, of the main distinction made by a kind of terminological fiat on pp. 94 and 100.

The most important passages are on pp. 94, 100 and 115. On p. 94 he speaks, rather sneeringly, of '"meaning" in the favourite philosophical sense of that word'; the implication is that if it would keep philosophers happy to go on using the word in this artificially restricted way, Austin does not object; he therefore adopts this terminology, but it is not to be taken as indicative of his own views about what is or is not part of meaning in a less artificially restricted sense.

On p. 99 he actually uses 'sense' to refer, apparently, to illocutionary force: 'it makes a great difference to our act in some sense – sense (B) – in which way and in which *sense* we were on this occasion "using" it'. Here the reference is to the illocutionary force (see p. 101); and on p. 99 itself advising, ordering, promising, etc., are given as examples.

On p. 100 he speaks in general of the current controversies about meaning and pleads for an extension of philosophers' attention beyond 'locutionary usage' to illocutionary force; the latter can, he says, be included in meaning, but he is going to use 'meaning' in the narrow sense of 'sense and reference' (no doubt to avoid confusion). He regards the word 'use' as just as bad as the word 'meaning'; both cover too many things which have to be distinguished.

On p. 148 he says

> We may well suspect that the theory of meaning as equivalent to 'sense and reference' will certainly require some weeding-out and reformulating in terms of the distinction between locutionary and illocutionary acts (*if this distinction is sound*: it is only adumbrated here). I admit that not enough has been done here: I have taken the old 'sense and reference' on the strength of current views; I would also stress that I have omitted any direct consideration of the illocutionary force of statements.

Bibliography

OF PUBLISHED PHILOSOPHICAL AND RELATED WORKS OF R. M. HARE

Papers are listed under the year in which they appeared, except that papers appearing in volumes of proceedings are listed under the year in which they were delivered. The numeration of entries within each year is arbitrary; FC indicates a forthcoming work.

1949:1 'Imperative Sentences', *Mind*, LVIII. Reprinted in this volume.
1950:1 Review of *Morality and God*, by E. W. Hirst, *Phil.*, xxv.
    2 Review of *Moral Obligation* and *Knowledge and Perception*, by H. A. Prichard, *Oxford Magazine*, LXVIII (15 June).
    3 'Theology and Falsification', *University*, 1. Reprinted in *New Essays in Philosophical Theology*, ed. A. G. N. Flew and A. MacIntyre (1955), and in *Religious Language*, ed. R. E. Santoni (1968) and other collections.
1951:1 '(Freedom of the Will', *Ar. Soc. Supp.*, xxv. Reprinted in FC: 3.
    2 Review of *The Philosophy of Plato*, by G. C. Field, *Mind*, LX.
    3 Review of *An Examination of the Place of Reason in Ethics*, by S. E. Toulmin, *Ph.Q.*, 1.
    4 Review of *Value: A Cooperative Inquiry*, ed. R. Lepley, *Mind*, LX.
1952:1 Review of *Morals and Revelation*, by H. D. Lewis, *Phil.*, XXVII.
    2 *The Language of Morals.*
1954:1 Review of *What is Value?*, by E. W. Hall, *Mind*, LXIII.
    2 Review of *The Ethics of Aristotle*, trans. J. A. K. Thompson, *Oxford Magazine*, LXXII (25 Feb).
    3 Review of *Philosophy and Psychoanalysis*, by J. Wisdom, *Phil.*, XXIX.
1955:1 'Universalisability', *Ar. Soc.*, LV (available also in Bobbs-Merrill reprints). Reprinted in FC: 3.
    2 'Ethics and Politics' (two articles and letters), *Listener* (Oct). First article reprinted in FC: 4.
    3 'Ética y Política' (Spanish trans. of 1955:2), *Revista Universidad de San Carlos*, XXXIII.
1956:1 Review of *Ethics*, by P. H. Nowell-Smith, *Phil.*, XXXI.
    2 Review of *Filosofia analitica e giurisprudenza*, by U. Scarpelli, *Mind*, LXV.
1957:1 'Geach: Good and Evil', *Analysis*, XVII 5 (available also in Bobbs-Merrill reprints). Reprinted in *Theories of Ethics*, ed. P. Foot (1967) and in FC: 3.
    2 'Oxford Moral Philosophy' (letters), *Listener* (21 Feb, 28 Mar).
    3 Review of *The Problem of Knowledge*, by A. J. Ayer, and *Logic and Knowledge*, by B. Russell, *Spectator* (4 Jan).

  4 Review of *British Philosophy in the Mid-Century*, ed. C. A. Mace, *Spectator*.
  5 'Are discoveries about the uses of words empirical?', *J. Phil.*, LIV (see 1960:1).
1957:6 Review of *Philosophical Analysis*, by J. O. Urmson, and *The Revolution in Philosophy*, by A. J. Ayer and others, *Phil. Rundschau*, V (in German).
  7 'Religion and Morals', in *Faith and Logic*, ed. B. G. Mitchell.
1959:1 'Broad's Approach to Moral Philosophy', in *The Philosophy of C. D. Broad*, ed. P. Schilpp. Reprinted in 1971:3.
1960:1 'Philosophical Discoveries' (the full version of 1957:5), *Mind*, LXIX. Reprinted in *The Linguistic Turn*, ed. R. Rorty (1967), *Plato's Meno*, ed. A. Sesonske and N. Fleming (1965), *Philosophy and Linguistics*, ed. C. Lyas (1971), and in 1971:3.
  2 'A School for Philosophers', *Ratio*, II (also in German ed.; translation errors corrected in later number). Reprinted in 1971:3.
  3 Review of *An Enquiry into Goodness*, by F. E. Sparshott, *Ph.Q.*, X.
  4 '"Rien n'a d'importance": l'anéantissement des valeurs est-il pensable?', in *La Philosophie Analytique*, ed. with Foreword by L. Beck; also discussion of other papers (Paris: Minuit). English version in FC:4.
  5 'Ethics', in *Encyclopedia of Western Philosophy and Philosophers*, ed. J. O. Urmson. Reprinted in FC:3.
1962:1 Review of *Generalization in Ethics*, by M. Singer, *Ph.Q.*, XII.
1963:1 *Freedom and Reason*.
  2 'Descriptivism', *Brit. Acad. Proc.*, XLIX. Reprinted in *The 'Is–Ought' Question*, ed. W. D. Hudson (1969), and in FC:3.
  3 Letter in *Times Lit. Supp.* (26 Apr) on review of *Freedom and Reason*.
1964:1 'Pain and Evil', *Ar. Soc. Supp.*, XXXVIII. Reprinted in *Moral Concepts*, ed. J. Feinberg (1969), and in FC:3.
  2 'Adolescents into Adults', in *Aims in Education*, ed. T. C. B. Hollins. Reprinted in FC:4.
  3 'A Question about Plato's Theory of Ideas', in *The Critical Approach: Essays in Honour of Karl Popper*, ed. M. Bunge. Reprinted in 1971:3.
  4 'The Promising Game', *Rev. Int. de Ph.*, LXX. Reprinted in *Theories of Ethics*, ed. P. Foot (1967), and in *The 'Is–Ought' Question*, ed. W. D. Hudson (1969).
  5 'Wat is Leven?', *Elseviers Weekblad* (19 Dec).
  6 'The Objectivity of Values', *Common Factor*, I.
1965:1 Review of *Norm and Action*, by G. H. von Wright, *Ph.Q.*, XV.
  2 'What is Life?', *Crucible* (English version of 1964:5). Reprinted in FC:4.
  3 'Plato and the Mathematicians', in *New Essays on Plato and Aristotle*, ed. R. Bambrough. Reprinted in 1971:3.
1966:1 'Peace', R.S.A. Lecture, Australian National University, Canberra, privately printed. Reprinted in FC:4.
1967:1 'The Lawful Government', in *Philosophy, Politics and Society*, 3rd series, ed. P. Laslett and W. G. Runciman. Reprinted in FC:4.
  2 'Conventional Morality', 'Decision', 'Deliberation', 'Ethics',

'Intention' and 'Right and Wrong', in *Dictionary of Christian Ethics*, ed. J. Macquarrie.
3 Review of *Freedom of the Individual*, by S. Hampshire, *Ph. Rev.*, LXXVI.
4 'Some Alleged Differences between Imperatives and Indicatives', *Mind*, LXXVI. Reprinted in this volume.

1968:1 Review of *Contemporary Moral Philosophy*, by G. J. Warnock, *Mind*, LXXVII.
2 Review of *The Concept of Education*, ed. R. S. Peters, *Mind*, LXXVII.
3 *Il linguaggio della morale* (Italian trans. of 1952:2).
4 'Wanting: Some Pitfalls', in 'Agent, Action and Reason': *Proc. of Univ. of W. Ontario Collqm.*, ed. R. Binkley (1971). Reprinted in this volume.

1969:1 'Practical Inferences', in *Festskrift til Alf Ross*, ed. V. Kruse (Copenhagen: Juristforbundets Forlag). Reprinted in this volume.
2 Review of *Directives and Norms*, by A. Ross, *Mind*, LXXVIII.
3 'Community and Communication', in *People and Cities*, ed. S. Verney. Reprinted in FC:4.
4 Review of *Law, Morality and Religion*, by B. G. Mitchell, *Phil.*, XLIV.
5 'Wissenschaft und praktische Philosophie', in *Proc.* of 9. Deutscher Kongress für Philosophie, Düsseldorf (forthcoming).

1970:1 'Meaning and Speech Acts', *Ph. Rev.*, LXXIX. Reprinted in this volume.
2 'Condizioni intellettuali per la sopravvivenza dell'uomo', *Proteus*, 1.
3 Reply to 'Liberals, Fanatics and Not-so-innocent Bystanders', by R. S. Katz, in *Jowett Papers, 1968–1969*, ed. Khanbhai *et al.*
4 General Introduction and Introduction to *Meno* in paperback edition of *The Dialogues of Plato*, trans. B. Jowett, ed. R. M. Hare and D. A. F. M. Russell (Sphere Books).

1971:1 Review of *The Prisoner and the Bomb*, by L. Van Der Post, *New York Review of Books*, XVII (20 May).
2 *Practical Inferences, and Other Essays*, containing 1949:1, 1967:4, 1969:1, 1970:1, 1971:2, 'Austin's Distinction between Locutionary and Illocutionary Acts', new appendices and bibliography.
3 *Essays on Philosophical Method*, containing 1959:1, 1960:1, 1960:2, 1964:3, 1965:3, 'The Practical Relevance of Philosophy' and 'The Argument from Received Opinion'.

Forthcoming (FC)
1 'The Simple Believer', in vol. of essays on religion and morality, ed. G. Outka and J. P. Reeder (Doubleday).
2 Italian trans. of 1950:3 and 1963:2 in vol. of essays, ed. G. Gava (Livania).
3 *Essays on the Moral Concepts*, containing 1951:1 (part), 1955:1, 1957:1, 1960:5, 1963:2, 1964:1, and 'Wrongness and Harm' (London, Macmillan).
4 *Applications of Moral Philosophy*, containing 1955:2 (part), 1960:4, 1964:2, 1965:2, 1966:1, 1967:1, 1969:3, 'Reasons of State' and 'Function and Tradition in Architecture' (London, Macmillan).

5 'Rules of War', in *Philosophy and Public Affairs*.
6 *Libertà e Ragione* (Italian trans. of 1963:1, Il Saggiatore II°).
7 *Die Sprache der Morao* (German trans. of 1952:2, Suhrkamp).
8 *Freiheit und Vernünft* (German trans. of 1963:1, Patmos).
9 Spanish trans. of 1952:2 (Instituto de Investigaciones Filosóficas de la Universidad Nacional Autónoma de México).

www.ingramcontent.com/pod-product-compliance
Lightning Source LLC
Chambersburg PA
CBHW021714230426
43668CB00008B/829